# Measurements

| Millimetres | Inches | Millimetres | Inches |
| --- | --- | --- | --- |
| 2mm | 1/16in | 13cm | 5in |
| 3mm | 1/8in | 13.5cm | 51/4in |
| 4mm | 1/6in | 15cm | 6in |
| 5mm | 1/4in | 16cm | 61/2in |
| 1cm | 1/2in | 18cm | 7in |
| 2cm | 3/4in | 19cm | 71/2in |
| 2.5cm | 1in | 20cm | 8in |
| 3cm | 11/4in | 23cm | 9in |
| 4cm | 11/2in | 24cm | 91/2in |
| 4.5cm | 13/4in | 25.5cm | 10in |
| 5cm | 2in | 28cm | 11in |
| 6cm | 21/2in | 30cm | 12in |
| 7.5cm | 3in | 32.5cm | 13in |
| 9cm | 31/2in | 35cm | 14in |
| 10cm | 4in | 37.5cm | 15in |

# Oven temperatures

| | Fan | Gas |
| --- | --- | --- |
| 110°C | 90°C | – |
| 120°C | 100°C | 1/2 |
| 140°C | 120°C | 1 |
| 150°C | 130°C | 2 |
| 160°C | 140°C | 3 |
| 180°C | 160°C | 4 |
| 190°C | 170°C | 5 |
| 200°C | 180°C | 6 |
| 220°C | 200°C | 7 |
| 230°C | 210°C | 8 |
| 240°C | 220°C | 9 |

# Sainsbury's
# Cookbook
## VOLUME TWO

# Sainsbury's
# Cookbook
## VOLUME TWO

# Welcome...

...to volume two of the Cookbook from Sainsbury's. We have brought together another great collection of recipes from the UK and around the world for you to try.

Each of the 150 recipes features readily available ingredients, clear step-by-step instructions and a photo to give you great results every time. Also included is information on key ingredients, cooking at Christmas and handy tips for making the most of your leftovers and preparing ahead – useful when time is short!

The recipes are divided into seven sections covering Starters and light bites through to Desserts and Cakes and bakes, including a dedicated Vegetarian chapter. There's also an index at the back to help you find the right recipe quickly.

Preparation and cooking times are provided for each recipe, along with the nutrition information. Whatever the occasion and whether you are cooking for family or friends, we hope you enjoy the recipes in this book.

## We've used these icons to make everything clear at a glance

 Suitable for vegetarians

 Recipes containing 1 or more of your 5-a-day, to help you plan for healthier eating. Try to eat at least 5 different portions of fruit and veg a day. Fresh, frozen, dried, canned and juice all count.

# Contents

# Starters and light bites

SERVES 4
PREP 10 minutes
COOK 1 hour 20 minutes

# French onion soup

This Parisian classic is given extra punch with a spoonful of brandy in every bowl. This soup is best enjoyed piping hot

2 tbsp olive oil
675g onions, thinly sliced
1 tsp granulated sugar
freshly ground black pepper
120ml red wine
2 tbsp plain flour
3 x 500g pouches of Signature beef stock by Sainsbury's
4 tbsp brandy (optional)

**FOR THE CROÛTES**
8 slices from a white baguette by Sainsbury's
1 garlic clove, halved
75g grated Gruyère or Emmental cheese by Sainsbury's

1 Melt the oil in a large, heavy-based pan over a low heat. Add the onions and sugar and turn to coat well. Season with black pepper and cook uncovered, stirring occasionally, for 40 minutes, or until the onions are a rich dark colour. Take care not to let them stick and burn.

2 Stir in the wine. Increase the heat to medium and stir for 5 minutes while the onions glaze. Sprinkle in the flour and stir for 2 minutes. Add the stock to the pan and bring to the boil. Reduce the heat to low, cover with a lid and simmer for 30 minutes.

3 Meanwhile, preheat the grill to a medium-high setting. To make the croûtes, rub the slices of baguette with the cut garlic and arrange them on a lightly oiled oven tray. Place the tray under the grill, toast on one side and turn. Sprinkle the grated cheese over the slices and return to the grill for 2–3 minutes, or until the cheese is melted and golden.

4 Divide the soup into 4 serving bowls and stir in 1 tablespoon of the brandy into each bowl, if using. Omit the brandy if serving to children.

5 Add 2 croûtes to the top of the soup in each bowl and serve immediately, piping hot.

**Per serving** 1691kJ/403kcal (20%), 14.3g fat (20%), 4.8g saturates (24%), 17.8g sugars (20%), 2.98g salt (50%)

**SERVES** 5
**PREP** 15 minutes
**COOK** 1 hour

# Allotment soup

This rustic soup from France combines an assortment of vegetables for a rich and tasty soup

2 tbsp olive oil
1 medium leek, finely sliced
1 small turnip, peeled
and diced into 1cm cubes
2 medium carrots, peeled and
diced into 1cm cubes
1 large courgette, diced
into 1cm cubes
1 celery stick, diced
into 1cm cubes

1 large potato, peeled
and diced into 1cm cubes
2 tomatoes, skinned
and diced into 1cm cubes
2 garlic cloves, finely chopped
2 litres vegetable stock
(made with 1 stock cube
and boiling water)

85g haricot beans from 410g
tin (drained weight 265g),
drained and rinsed
175g Basics green beans
by Sainsbury's, cut into
2cm lengths

**1** Heat the oil in a large pan, and add the leek, turnip, carrots, courgette, celery, potato, tomatoes and garlic. Cook, stirring often, for 10-15 minutes, or until the vegetables are soft but not brown.

**2** Add the stock, season with black pepper and bring to a brisk simmer, then cover, reduce the heat and cook at a gentle simmer for 40 minutes, or until the vegetables are tender. If more liquid is required add some boiling water.

**3** Add the haricot beans to the large pan, along with the green beans and cook for 3-4 minutes, or until tender.

**Per serving** 719kJ/171kcal (9%), 5.1g fat (7%), 0.8g saturates (4%), 6.8g sugars (8%), 0.09g salt (2%)

# Porcini mushroom soup

This Italian country soup has deep, earthy flavours from the delicious mix of mushrooms

30g dried porcini mushrooms by Sainsbury's
1 tbsp olive oil, plus extra to serve
2 onions, finely chopped
2 tsp chopped rosemary leaves, washed
1 tsp fresh thyme leaves, washed

2 garlic cloves, finely sliced
115g chestnut mushrooms, sliced
2 celery sticks with leaves, washed and finely chopped
390g carton chopped tomatoes by Sainsbury's
750ml vegetable stock (made with 1 stock cube and boiling water)

freshly ground black pepper
½ day-old ciabatta or small crusty white loaf, torn into chunks

1  Put the dried porcini in a heatproof bowl, pour over 300ml boiling water and leave to stand for 30 minutes. Drain, reserving the soaking liquid. Chop any large pieces of porcini.

2  Heat the oil in a pan, add the onions, cover and leave to cook for 10 minutes, or until soft. Add the rosemary, thyme, garlic, chestnut mushrooms and celery and continue cooking, uncovered, until the celery has softened.

3  Add the tomatoes, porcini and the stock. Strain the soaking liquid through a fine sieve into the pan. Bring the soup to the boil, then reduce the heat and simmer gently for 45 minutes.

4  Season with black pepper and add the chunks of bread. Remove the pan from the heat. Cover and leave to stand for 10 minutes before serving. Spoon into bowls, drizzle each serving with a little olive oil and serve immediately.

**Per serving** 975kJ/232kcal (12%), 7.8g fat (11%), 1.4g saturates (7%), 11.2g sugars (12%), 1.49g salt (25%)

# Chickpea, red rice and artichoke salad

This recipe uses a variety of rice cultivated in the Camargue region of southern France. The rice has a slightly nutty taste that makes this salad great to eat on its own or as a side dish with grilled meat or fish

400g French Camargue red rice by Sainsbury's
400g tin chickpeas, drained and rinsed
290g jar chargrilled artichokes in olive oil by Sainsbury's, drained and oil reserved
1 red chilli, deseeded and finely chopped
handful of fresh coriander, washed and finely chopped

handful of fresh flat-leaf parsley, washed and finely chopped
2 tbsp pine nuts, toasted
75g feta cheese by Sainsbury's, crumbled

**FOR THE CORIANDER AND ORANGE DRESSING**
2 tbsp oil reserved from artichokes, or 2 tbsp extra virgin olive oil

1 tbsp white wine vinegar
1 orange, juice only
1 tsp coriander seeds, lightly crushed
$1/2$ tsp Dijon mustard
pinch of sugar
freshly ground black pepper

1 For the dressing, place all the ingredients in a small bowl or jug and mix well. Season with black pepper.

2 Cook the rice according to the pack instructions. Drain well and transfer to a serving bowl.

3 While the rice is still warm, stir through the chickpeas, artichokes, chilli and herbs, and mix well. Pour the dressing over the rice mixture and toss together. Top with the pine nuts and feta cheese and serve.

**Per serving** 1504kJ/361kcal (18%), 24.2g fat (35%), 5.9g saturates (30%), 3.6g sugars (4%), 1.46g salt (24%)

SERVES 6
PREP 20 minutes
COOK 15 minutes

# Grilled mushrooms with goat's cheese

The grilled slices of bread or croûtes should be about the same size as the mushrooms, so choose an appropriately sized loaf

400g baguette
1 tbsp olive oil, for brushing
250g pack large flat
mushrooms by Sainsbury's
100g French chevre blanc
goat's cheese
1 tbsp balsamic vinegar,
for drizzling
freshly ground black pepper
12 black olives, pitted
and chopped

**FOR THE DRESSING**
1 tbsp thyme leaves, washed
1 tbsp balsamic vinegar
2 tbsp extra virgin olive oil
1 tsp Dijon mustard
1 garlic clove, chopped

1 Preheat the oven to 180°C/160°C fan/gas 4. To make the dressing, whisk together all the ingredients and set aside.

2 Cut the bread diagonally into 1cm slices. Brush both sides with olive oil and place on an oven tray. Bake for 10 minutes, turning halfway through cooking, until crisp and golden.

3 Remove the stems from the mushrooms. Slice the goat's cheese into rounds. Place a slice in each mushroom cap. Preheat the grill to a medium setting, then place the mushrooms on a grill pan. Drizzle with balsamic vinegar, then season with black pepper. Place the mushrooms under the grill for 5 minutes, or until the goat's cheese is bubbling and the mushrooms are tender.

4 To serve, place each croûte on a serving plate, top with a grilled mushroom and some chopped olives and drizzle with the dressing. Serve while still hot.

**Per serving** 1330kJ/317kcal (16%), 12.0g fat (17%), 4.1g saturates (21%), 4.1g sugars (5%), 1.59g salt (27%)

**Why not try?**
To make blue cheese mushrooms, use a blue cheese, such as blue Stilton or Cambozola by Sainsbury's.

# Mushrooms

**< Porcini** is regarded as a chef's favourite, valued for its smooth, creamy flesh, rich, savoury flavour and classic fairytale shape. Also available dried for a more intense flavour. Delicious sautéed or added to risotto and pasta dishes.

**^ Large flat** mushrooms are fully grown button mushrooms. They have a firm texture and earthy flavour, and are delicious grilled, pan-fried, stuffed or roasted.

**< Shiitake** mushrooms have a faintly woody flavour and chewy texture, ideal for stir-frying or adding to soups. They are available fresh or dried.

**> Buna-Shimeji** is an attractive Japanese clumping mushroom with a nutty flavour and crisp texture. They are bitter when raw, so should always be cooked.

**^ Oyster** mushrooms are so-called because their shape resembles an oyster shell. They are tender and mildly flavoured, with a hint of aniseed. Use in stir-fries and Asian-style soups.

^ **Enoki** have a crisp texture and mild flavour. Cultivated in clumps, they look beautiful cooked in soups and stir-fries, or used raw in salads and sandwiches.

^ **Portobello** is a large, meaty variety of mushroom with firm flesh and a full-bodied flavour. The generous size makes it perfect as a meat replacement in burgers. Also available dried.

^ **Button** mushrooms have a very mild flavour that benefits from sautéing in a little oil or butter. They can also be used raw in salads and as crudités.

> **White closed cup** mushrooms are button mushrooms that have been allowed to mature for longer. They have a similarly mild flavour and firm texture, and work well whole or quartered in stews or hotpots.

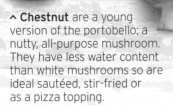

^ **Chestnut** are a young version of the portobello; a nutty, all-purpose mushroom. They have less water content than white mushrooms so are ideal sautéed, stir-fried or as a pizza topping.

## Storing and preparing

Fresh mushrooms can be kept in the fridge in a closed paper bag for up to a week. To prepare, wipe them with kitchen paper before carefully twisting and removing the stalks. Larger varieties may benefit from peeling; for smaller, more tender varieties, you can leave the stalk in. Dried mushrooms have a more intense flavour, and can be added to stocks, soups or stews.

# Mixed mushroom tart

This recipe can be made with different types of mushrooms, allowing you to experiment with more unusual varieties

250g ready rolled light
shortcrust pastry
by Sainsbury's
plain flour, for dusting
2 eggs, plus 1 lightly beaten
25g unsalted butter
200g pack British speciality
mushrooms by Sainsbury's or
a selection of oyster, enoki,
shiitake or Portobello
mushrooms, roughly chopped

140g chestnut mushrooms,
roughly chopped
3 garlic cloves, grated
or finely chopped
freshly ground black pepper
2 handfuls of spinach leaves,
roughly chopped
150ml half-fat crème fraîche
3 tsp whole milk

**1** Preheat the oven to 200°C/180°C fan/gas 6. Use the pastry to line a 12 x 35 cm rectangular loose-bottomed tart tin. Trim away the excess, line the pastry case with greaseproof & non-stick baking paper by Sainsbury's, and fill with ceramic baking beans.

**2** Bake in the oven for 15-20 minutes until the edges are golden. Remove the beans and paper, brush the bottom of the case with a little of the beaten egg and return to the oven for 2-3 minutes to crisp. Remove from the oven and set aside. Reduce the oven temperature to 180°C/160°C fan/gas 4.

**3** Heat the butter in a large, deep frying pan over a low heat. Add the mushrooms and garlic, and season with black pepper. Cook, stirring occasionally, for about 10 minutes until the mushrooms release their juices. Tip in the spinach and cook, stirring, for a further 5 minutes until just wilted. Spoon the mixture into the pastry case.

**4** Mix the crème fraîche, milk and eggs together, and season with black pepper. Carefully pour this mixture over the mushroom filling. Grind over a little black pepper and bake in the oven for 15-20 minutes until set. Leave to cool for 10 minutes before releasing from the tin. Serve hot or cold.

**Per serving** 1368kJ/328 kcal (16%), 20g fat (29%), 9.2g saturates (46%), 2.9g sugars (3%), 0.28g salt (5%)

**Cook's tip**
The remaining pastry from the block can be frozen. It should be used within 1 month. Defrost overnight in the fridge. Do not refreeze.

# Trio of Mediterranean dips

Serve these classic dips with crudités or split and toasted pittas

**BABA GANOUSH**
oil, for greasing
900g aubergines, cut in
half lengthways
2 large garlic cloves, crushed
2 tbsp extra virgin olive oil
2 tbsp low-fat
Greek-style yogurt
3 tbsp tahini paste by
Sainsbury's, plus extra to taste
1 lemon, juice only, plus extra
to taste

freshly ground black pepper
sprigs of fresh coriander,
washed, to garnish

**HOUMOUS**
400g tin chickpeas in water
by Sainsbury's
3 tbsp tahini paste
3 lemons, juice only
3 garlic cloves, chopped
2 tsp paprika, for sprinkling
1 tbsp olive oil, for drizzling

**TZATZIKI**
1 large cucumber
sea salt and freshly ground
black pepper
300ml Greek-style yogurt
1 tbsp olive oil
1 garlic clove, grated
or finely chopped
few fronds of dill or mint leaves,
washed and snipped
1 tbsp lemon juice

## Baba ganoush  SERVES 6 PREP 10 minutes, plus standing COOK 25-30 minutes

1 Preheat the oven to 220°C/200°C fan/gas 7. Lightly grease a baking sheet. Score down the centre of each aubergine half without cutting through the skin, then place on the baking sheet, cut-sides down. Bake for 25-30 minutes, or until the flesh is softened. Place the aubergine halves in a colander and leave for 15 minutes.

2 Scoop the aubergine flesh into a blender or food processor. Add the garlic, oil, yogurt, tahini and lemon juice, and process until smooth. Taste and adjust the tahini and lemon juice, if needed, then season with black pepper. Garnish with coriander, and serve.

**Per serving** 499kJ/120kcal (6%), 9.1g fat (13%), 1.3g saturates (7%), 3.9g sugars (4%), 0.03g salt (<1%)

## Houmous SERVES 4 PREP 10 minutes

1 Drain the chickpeas, reserving 4-6 tablespoons of the liquid from the tin. Place the chickpeas in a blender or food processor with 3 tablespoons of the reserved liquid.

2 Add the tahini, lemon juice and garlic, then blend until smooth and creamy. Add a little more of the reserved liquid, if required. Serve sprinkled with paprika and drizzled with oil.

**Per serving** 736kJ/177kcal (9%), 10.3g fat (15%), 1.5g saturates (8%), 0.6g sugars (<1%), <0.01g salt (<1%)

## Tzatziki SERVES 6 PREP 10-15 minutes, plus soaking and standing

1 Peel the cucumber, leaving a few narrow strips unpeeled, and cut into two. Cut each piece in half lengthways. Scoop out and discard the seeds. Finely chop the cucumber and place in a colander. Sprinkle 1 teaspoon of salt over the cucumber and mix in. Leave to drain for at least 20 minutes and rinse thoroughly. Press down with the palm of your hands and pat dry with kitchen paper.

2 Place the yogurt in a bowl, stir in the oil and garlic and fold in the cucumber. Stir in the dill or mint, season with black pepper and add the lemon juice. Let stand for 10 minutes then serve.

**Per serving** 200kJ/48kcal (2%), 1.7g fat (2%), 0.4g saturates (2%), 3.5g sugars (4%), 0.09g salt (2%)

# Chorizo, chickpea and mango salad

Choose a full-flavoured, spicy chorizo for this dish; it will complement the chickpeas

1 tbsp olive oil
60g chorizo sausage from Sainsbury's deli counter, cut into thick slices
400g tin chickpeas, drained and rinsed
3 garlic cloves, finely chopped
handful of fresh flat-leaf parsley, washed and finely chopped
1 tbsp dry sherry
2 ripe mangoes, stoned and flesh diced

small handful of fresh basil, washed and roughly chopped
small handful of fresh mint leaves, washed and roughly chopped
small handful of fresh coriander leaves, washed and roughly chopped
200g bag young leaf spinach

1  Heat the olive oil in a frying pan, add the chorizo and chickpeas and cook over a low heat for 1 minute, then add the garlic and parsley and cook for a further minute. Add the sherry and cook for 10 minutes, stirring occasionally.

2  Put the mango and remaining herbs in a bowl and toss together, then add the chickpea mixture and combine well. Spoon onto a bed of spinach to serve.

**Per serving** 1912kJ/457kcal (23%), 19.6g fat (28%), 5g saturates (25%), 23.5g sugars (26%), 1.05g salt (18%)

# Seared tuna niçoise

Although traditionally served without potatoes, the addition of small, warm salad potatoes enhances this classic salad

300g small salad
potatoes, halved
100g dwarf green beans by
Sainsbury's, halved
2 x 200g packs tuna steaks
by Sainsbury's
freshly ground black pepper

16 cherry tomatoes, halved
200g bag of mixed leaf salad
by Sainsbury's
4 hard-boiled eggs, peeled
and quartered
50g Basics black pitted olives
by Sainsbury's

**FOR THE DRESSING**
3 tbsp olive oil, plus extra
for brushing
1 ½ tbsp red wine vinegar
1 tsp caster sugar
1 heaped tsp Dijon mustard
freshly ground black pepper

1 Cook the potatoes in a large pan of boiling water for 20 minutes, or until tender. Drain.

2 Meanwhile, make the dressing in a large bowl. Whisk together the oil, vinegar, sugar and mustard, and season with black pepper. Cook the beans in a pan of boiling water for 2–3 minutes until just tender. Drain the beans using a colander, refresh under cold water and drain again.

3 When the potatoes are ready, heat a large frying pan. Brush the tuna with a little oil and season with black pepper. Cook over a high heat for 2–3 minutes on each side or until cooked through, opaque and flakes easily. Rest the fish, covered, while you finish the salad.

4 Put the warm potatoes into the dressing and mix until thoroughly coated. Add the beans, tomatoes and salad leaves and toss them all together.

5 Serve the salad on a platter, or individual plates. Place the egg around, scatter the olives over and top with tuna, sliced into pieces.

**Per serving** 1639kJ/391kcal (20%), 15.4g fat (22%), 3.1g saturates (16%), 6.6g sugars (7%), 0.71g salt (12%)

# Braised lentils

This dish works well on its own, but makes a good alternative side dish when served with sausages or pork

1 tbsp olive oil
1 onion, finely chopped
1 large carrot, finely chopped
1 celery stick, finely chopped
1 garlic clove, finely chopped
1 heaped tbsp plain flour
500g pouch Signature vegetable stock by Sainsbury's

2 x 380g cartons SO Organic green lentils by Sainsbury's, drained
freshly ground black pepper
½ x 400g baguette, torn into 4 chunks, to serve

1  Heat the oil in a large, heavy-based saucepan. Cook the onion, carrot and celery for 7-10 minutes until softened, but not browned. Add the garlic and cook for a further minute.

2  Sprinkle over the flour, stir it in and cook for a further minute or 2, before stirring in the stock and 100ml water.

3  Add the lentils and season to taste. Bring them to a brisk simmer, then reduce the heat to a gentle simmer and cook for 7-10 minutes until the lentils are soft and the sauce has thickened slightly. Serve hot with crusty bread.

**Per serving** 1441kJ/341kcal (17%), 4.9g fat (7%), 1.6g saturates (8%), 6.9g sugars (8%), 1.67g salt (28%)

### Get ahead
Prepare double or triple quantities and freeze in family-sized portions in separate freezer bags.

SERVES 4
PREP 25 minutes
COOK 15 minutes

# Scotch eggs

A firm favourite for picnics and packed lunches. Tastes great with a spoonful of caramelised onion chutney

3 spring onions, finely chopped
325g pork sausagemeat
by Sainsbury's
pinch of crushed chilli flakes
2 tsp dried mixed herbs
freshly ground black pepper
4 hard-boiled eggs, shelled

25g plain flour
500ml sunflower oil,
for deep-frying
1 egg, beaten
100g dried golden
breadcrumbs

1 In a large bowl, mix together the spring onions, sausagemeat, chilli flakes and herbs, and season with black pepper.

2 Coat the eggs in flour, then quarter the sausagemeat mixture, flatten it out and place an egg in the centre of each piece. Using your hands, gather up the mixture to totally encase the egg.

3 Pour oil into a large saucepan (it should be enough to just cover the eggs when deep-frying) and heat to approximately 190°C, or until a cube of bread dropped in sizzles and turns golden within 1 minute. Place the beaten egg and the breadcrumbs on separate plates. Dip each Scotch egg into the beaten egg, then into the breadcrumbs.

4 Carefully place in the hot oil two at a time, making sure that the eggs are immersed in the oil. Fry for 2-3 minutes, or until golden and cooked through with no pink remaining. Remove from the oil with a slotted spoon. Drain on kitchen paper and leave to cool on a wire rack.

**Per serving** 3010kJ/726kcal (36%), 56.8g fat (81%), 14.6g saturates (73%), 2.1g sugars (2%), 1.59g salt (27%)

## Why not try?

Try making vegetarian Scotch eggs. Instead of the sausagemeat, place a **410g tin of haricot beans by Sainsbury's**, drained and rinsed, in a food processor with **60g French goat's cheese by Sainsbury's** and process until smooth. Transfer to a large bowl, add **spring onions, chilli flakes, mixed herbs** and **3 tbsp of dried breadcrumbs**. Coat and shape the mixture around the egg, then continue with the recipe as above from step 3.

# Fish

**SERVES** 4
**PREP** 5 minutes
**COOK** 10-15 minutes

# Baked fish with a herb crust

This easy fish recipe is an aromatic treat and looks amazing with its vivid green crust

50g fresh white breadcrumbs, from day old farmhouse loaf by Sainsbury's
2 tbsp fresh basil leaves, roughly chopped
2 tbsp fresh flat-leaf parsley leaves, roughly chopped
2 tbsp fresh chives, roughly chopped

$^1/_2$ lemon, grated zest
freshly ground black pepper
3 tbsp olive oil, plus extra for brushing
4 fillets firm-fleshed white fish, such as cod or haddock (about 150g each), from Sainsbury's fish counter

**TO SERVE**
500g baby potatoes, larger ones halved
300g dwarf green beans by Sainsbury's

1 Preheat the oven to 220°C/200°C fan/gas 7.

2 Using a hand blender or a small food processor, whizz the breadcrumbs, herbs, lemon zest and black pepper, to taste, until the breadcrumbs are bright green.

3 Add the oil gradually, with the food processor still running, until the mixture comes together to form a thick, bright green paste.

4 Cook the potatoes in plenty of boiling water until just tender, 10-15 minutes depending on their size. In a separate pan, cook the beans in boiling water for 5-7 minutes until just tender but still crisp.

5 Meanwhile, brush the fish fillets with a little oil on both sides and season with black pepper. Press the herby crust on to the top (or skinless side) of the fillets, packing it down well. Place on a non-stick oven tray and bake in the top of the oven for 10 minutes, or until the fish are cooked through, opaque, flake easily and are turning crispy on top. Serve with the potatoes and beans.

**Per serving** 1644kJ/391kcal (20%), 10.5g fat (15%), 1.7g saturates (9%), 4.5g sugars (5%), 0.56g salt (9%)

## Cook's tip
Use up extra herbs by making larger quantities of this breadcrumb mix and simply freeze in a sturdy freezer bag for up to 2 months. The breadcrumbs can be used straight from the freezer.

# Green prawn curry

This aromatic, Thai-style curry is served with dill to balance
the intense flavour of the lime leaves

2 tbsp sunflower oil

4 tbsp Thai green curry paste
by Sainsbury's

1 tbsp shrimp paste

1 tbsp palm or granulated sugar

400ml tin coconut milk light
by Sainsbury's

250ml chicken or
vegetable stock (made with
½ stock cube and boiling water)

4-6 kaffir lime leaves, bruised

Thai fish sauce, to taste

2 large waxy potatoes, such as
Charlotte or Anya, peeled and
cut into 2.5cm pieces

2 x 225g packs frozen raw
jumbo king prawns by
Sainsbury's, defrosted and
patted dry with kitchen paper

1 bunch of dill, washed
and chopped, to serve

1 Heat the oil in a pan over a medium-high heat and stir-fry the curry paste for about
2 minutes or until fragrant. Add the shrimp paste and sugar, and stir-fry for 1 minute.

2 Reduce the heat and add the coconut milk, stock, kaffir lime leaves and fish sauce,
and stir to combine. Add the potatoes, cover and cook for 20 minutes.

3 Add the prawns and stir well, then cover again and cook for about 5 minutes,
or until they turn pink and are cooked through, adding more liquid if necessary.
Sprinkle with the chopped dill and serve.

**Per serving** 1205kJ/288kcal (14%), 15.3g fat (22%), 8.1g saturates (41%),
9.4g sugars (10%), 5.18g salt (86%)

### Get ahead
Make the curry base to the end of step 2 up
to 2 days ahead, cover and refrigerate. Reheat gently
but thoroughly before continuing with step 3.

# Salmon and potato gratin

This gratin, infused with the delicate aniseed flavour of dill, makes a simple and delicious midweek meal

1kg Charlotte or Anya potatoes
5g sunflower spread
2 heaped tbsp finely
chopped dill
400g pack Basics skinless
salmon fillets by Sainsbury's,
cut into 2cm chunks

freshly ground black pepper
150ml single cream
150ml fish or vegetable stock
(made with $^1/_2$ stock cube and
boiling water)

1 Preheat the oven to 190°C/170°C fan/gas 5. Cut the potatoes into 5mm-thick slices. Bring them to the boil in a large pan of boiling water and simmer for 5 minutes until part-cooked. Drain well. Rub a 25cm ovenproof dish with the sunflower spread.

2 Layer half the potato slices in the dish. Sprinkle the dill on the potatoes, lay the salmon over in a single layer and season with black pepper. Top with the rest of the potatoes, making sure that the final layer looks neat.

3 Whisk the cream and stock together, pour it over the potatoes and cook for 50 minutes to 1 hour, or until the top is crispy, the salmon flakes easily and the potatoes are cooked through.

**Per serving** 1969kJ/470kcal (24%), 19.9g fat (28%), 7.9g saturates (40%), 4.9g sugars (5%), 0.82g salt (14%)

# Fish pie

Create this versatile dish using your favourite fish. Topping it with pastry, rather than mash, speeds up the cooking time

300g skinless salmon fillet, from Sainsbury's fish counter

200g skinless smoked haddock fillet, from Sainsbury's fish counter

50g sunflower spread

5 tbsp plain flour, plus extra for dusting

350ml semi-skimmed milk

freshly ground black pepper

pinch of grated nutmeg

200g pack MSC peeled prawns by Sainsbury's

100g bag young leaf spinach

250g ready rolled light puff pastry by Sainsbury's

1 egg, lightly beaten, for glazing

**1** Preheat the oven to 200°C/180°C fan/gas 6. Poach the salmon and haddock in simmering water for 5 minutes. Drain, cover and cool.

**2** Melt the sunflower spread in a pan. Remove from the heat and whisk in the flour until a paste is formed. Gradually add the milk, whisking to avoid any lumps. Season with black pepper and add the nutmeg. Bring the sauce to the boil, reduce the heat and cook for 5 minutes, stirring.

**3** Flake the fish into a bowl and add the prawns. Spread the uncooked spinach over the top and pour the hot sauce over it. When the spinach has wilted, mix the filling together and transfer to a 18cm pie dish.

**4** On a floured surface, cut the pastry to a shape slightly bigger than the pie dish, reserving the strips of leftover pastry. Brush the rim of the dish with some egg and press the pastry strips around the rim.

**5** Brush the edging with egg and top with the pastry lid. Press down to seal the lid, and trim off any overhang. Brush the top with egg and cut 2 slits in it. Bake in the top of the oven for 20-25 minutes until golden, and allow to rest for 5 minutes before serving.

**Per serving** 2644kJ/631kcal (32%), 28.5g fat (41%), 9.3g saturates (47%), 6.1g sugars (7%), 2.1g salt (35%)

## Get ahead

Leave the pie until cold, then cover, chill overnight and reheat the next day. Make sure it is piping hot in the centre, and cover the top with foil if the pastry is becoming too dark.

# Baked tuna with cherry tomatoes

Use really ripe tomatoes for this dish and they will partially break down to make an instant sauce

4 tuna steaks (about 150g each),
from Sainsbury's fish counter
freshly ground black pepper
½ lime, zest and juice
2 garlic cloves, finely chopped
200g cherry tomatoes, halved
150ml dry white wine
200g low-fat natural yogurt
3 tbsp chopped coriander
leaves, washed

**TO SERVE**
500g baby potatoes,
larger ones halved
1 tbsp olive oil
300g dwarf green beans
by Sainsbury's

**1** Preheat the oven to 180°C/160°C fan/gas 4. Add the potatoes to a large pan of boiling water, bring back to the boil and cook for 5 minutes. Drain and tip back into the pan and shake well to slightly roughen. Put on an oven tray and toss in the oil.

**2** Place the tuna steaks in a single layer in a shallow ovenproof dish. Season with black pepper and sprinkle with the lime zest.

**3** Arrange the chopped garlic and tomatoes over and around the fish. Pour the wine into the dish and cover tightly with foil. Place both the tuna steaks and the potatoes in the oven, and bake for 20-25 minutes.

**4** Meanwhile, put the yogurt, lime juice and coriander in a small serving dish, season with black pepper and stir well. Cook the beans in a pan of boiling water for 5-7 minutes until just tender but still crisp.

**5** Remove the tuna steaks from the dish and place on warm serving plates. Arrange a few tomatoes on each plate and spoon over some of the cooking juices. Serve with the coriander and lime sauce, roasted potatoes and beans.

**Per serving** 1700kJ/403kcal (20%), 6.2g fat (9%), 1.9g saturates (10%), 9.4g sugars (10%), 0.31g salt (5%)

**Why not try?**
Instead of tuna, this also works well with haddock or cod fillet, or any fish with a firm texture.

# Cheese-crusted salmon

The cheese coating adds real flavour to the salmon; it is like a rarebit mixture roasted with the fish and is a great way to get children to eat fish

2 x 240g packs Scottish
salmon fillets by Sainsbury's
oil, for greasing
freshly ground black pepper
75g lighter mature Cheddar
cheese by Sainsbury's, grated
15g Basics Italian hard cheese
by Sainsbury's, grated

1 tsp Worcestershire sauce
by Sainsbury's
2 slices wholemeal loaf, whizzed
into breadcrumbs
2 x 170g bags Italian-style salad
by Sainsbury's, to serve

1 Preheat the oven to 200°C/180°C fan/gas 6. Sit the fish in a large, lightly oiled roasting tin, and season with black pepper.

2 Mix together the cheeses, Worcestershire sauce and breadcrumbs, then spoon equal amounts onto each salmon fillet.

3 Press the mixture evenly onto the fillets to coat and bake in the oven for 20-25 minutes, or until the top begins to turn golden and the fish is flaky and cooked through. Cover with foil if it starts to cook too quickly. Remove and serve with a green salad.

**Per serving** 1796kJ/430kcal (22%), 25.2g fat (36%), 6.4g saturates (32%), 2.5g sugars (3%), 0.8g salt (13%)

### Cook's tip
Try to get large loin fillets for this dish, which are thicker than the tail. If using tail fillets you may need to reduce the baking time.

SERVES 2
PREP 20 minutes
COOK 50-65 minutes,
plus resting

# Crab, prawn and saffron tart

The delicate flavours of crab and prawns balance wonderfully with the unusual taste of the saffron

100g ready rolled light shortcrust pastry by Sainsbury's
plain flour, for dusting
pinch of saffron threads
100g pack white and brown crab meat by Sainsbury's
125g MSC peeled prawns by Sainsbury's

200ml half-fat crème fraîche
1 egg
1 tbsp finely chopped tarragon or chervil
freshly ground black pepper
2 x 170g bags Italian-style salad by Sainsbury's, to serve

1 Preheat the oven to 200°C/180°C fan/gas 6. Cut the pastry into a large circle and use to line a 15cm loose-bottomed tart tin, pressing it into the corners. Ensure it overlaps the sides by at least 2cm. Prick the bottom with a fork. Line with greaseproof & non-stick baking paper by Sainsbury's, and fill with ceramic baking beans.

2 Place the tart tin on a baking sheet and bake in the centre of the oven for 20-25 minutes. Remove the beans and paper. Bake for 5 minutes to crisp the bottom. Remove from the oven and leave to cool. Reduce the heat to 180°C/160°C fan/gas 4.

3 Splash 1 tablespoon boiling water over the saffron in a small bowl to allow the colour to develop. Put the crab meat and prawns in a sieve over a sink and press down to remove any excess water. Toss together and scatter over the pastry base.

4 Whisk the crème fraîche and egg in a jug. Add the herbs, the saffron and its soaking water, season with black pepper and mix well. Put the tart tin on a baking sheet, and pour the egg mix over the tart filling. Bake in the middle of the oven for 30-35 minutes until golden. Remove from the oven and leave for 10 minutes. Trim off the overhanging pastry edges with a knife, remove the tart from the tin and serve warm or cold with salad.

Per serving 2337kJ/560kcal (28%), 31.6g fat (45%), 15.7g saturates (79%), 5.4g sugars (6%), 2.17g salt (36%)

Cook's tip
The remaining pastry from the block can be frozen. It should be used within 1 month. Defrost at room temperature for 1 hour, or overnight in the fridge. Do not refreeze.

# Keralan fish curry

The flavour and aroma of this exotic curry is subtle and fragrant.
Try it with any firm white fish

800g skinless haddock fillets,
from Sainsbury's fish counter,
cut into bite-sized pieces
2 tsp ground turmeric
freshly ground black pepper
1 tbsp vegetable oil
1 large onion, finely sliced
1 tsp black mustard seeds
5 curry leaves

4cm piece fresh root ginger,
peeled and finely chopped
2 tbsp tamarind paste
by Sainsbury's
200ml coconut milk light
by Sainsbury's
2 spring onions, finely sliced
1 red chilli, deseeded and
finely chopped (optional)

**TO SERVE**
300g basmati rice, cooked
according to pack instructions
a small bunch of fresh coriander,
washed and chopped

1  Place the haddock in a bowl, sprinkle with the turmeric, season with black pepper
and stir to coat. Cover and set aside for 15 minutes.

2  Heat the oil in a large, non-stick frying pan over a medium heat, and add the onion,
black mustard seeds and curry leaves. Fry gently for 10 minutes, stirring occasionally,
until the onion is lightly golden.

3  Add the ginger and cook for 1 or 2 minutes, then add the tamarind paste, coconut
milk and 150ml hot water, and stir well. Heat the sauce to a gentle simmer.

4  Add the fish and simmer gently for 3–4 minutes, or until it is cooked through
and flakes easily. Stir in the spring onions and chilli (if using).

5  Serve the curry with basmati rice, sprinkled with chopped coriander leaves.

**Per serving** 2609kJ/617kcal (31%), 10g fat (14%), 4g saturates (20%),
7g sugars (8%), 1.16g salt (19%)

🕐 **Get ahead**
Make the sauce (following steps 2 and 3)
up to 2 days in advance, cover and refrigerate.
Prepare the fish following step 1. Reheat the sauce
gently until it is hot (do not boil or it may split,
because of the coconut milk), and continue to
follow from step 4.

# Salmon salsa verde

A simple, piquant meal that takes just minutes to prepare

2 x 240g packs Scottish salmon
fillets by Sainsbury's
3 tbsp extra virgin olive oil, plus
extra for rubbing
freshly ground black pepper
15g fresh basil leaves, washed
15g fresh flat-leaf parsley
leaves, washed

15g fresh mint leaves, washed
1 lemon, juice only
4 anchovy fillets in olive oil by
Sainsbury's, drained
1 tbsp capers by Sainsbury's,
rinsed
2 tsp Dijon mustard
1 garlic clove, crushed

**FOR THE CRUSHED POTATOES**
1kg Maris Piper or King Edward
potatoes, washed and cut
into chunks
freshly ground black pepper

1 Preheat the grill on its highest setting. Rub the salmon with a little oil and season it with black pepper on both sides. Grill it for 3-5 minutes on each side (depending on thickness), until it is opaque and flakes easily.

2 Meanwhile, place the potatoes in a large pan, cover with cold water and bring to the boil. Cook for 10-15 minutes until tender. Drain, roughly mash together and season with black pepper.

3 While the fish and potatoes are cooking, make the salsa verde. Put all the remaining ingredients except the oil into the bowl of a small food processor, and whizz to a rough paste. Add the oil gradually, with the food processor still running, until the mixture comes together to form a thick, bright green sauce.

4 Serve the fish on the mashed potato with the salsa verde spooned over.

**Per serving** 2208kJ/527kcal (26%), 22.4g fat (32%), 4.8g saturates (24%), 2g sugars (2%), 1.11g salt (19%)

### Cook's tip
Try doubling or tripling this salsa verde recipe, to use up extra herbs. The sauce will store in a jar with a tightly fitting lid in the fridge for up to 2 days, and can be used on grilled meats, in sandwiches, or even mixed into mayonnaise for an instant dip for crudités or dressing for a warm potato salad.

SERVES 4 (2 per serving)
PREP 40 minutes,
plus chilling
COOK 20 minutes

# Haddock fish cakes

Japanese panko breadcrumbs give these fishcakes a wonderfully crispy finish. Smoked mackerel can be used instead of the haddock

500g Maris Piper
potatoes, peeled
2 tbsp unsalted butter
freshly ground black pepper
1 tbsp olive oil
1 leek, finely chopped
400g skinless undyed smoked
haddock from Sainsbury's
fish counter
4 tbsp finely chopped flat-leaf
parsley leaves

1 lemon, grated zest
1 heaped tbsp capers, rinsed,
dried and roughly chopped
50g plain flour
1 egg, lightly beaten
75g panko breadcrumbs
or day-old breadcrumbs
1 ½ tbsp sunflower oil,
for shallow frying

**TO SERVE**
60ml lighter mayonnaise
by Sainsbury's
2 heaped tbsp capers
1 tbsp chopped parsley, washed
½ lemon, zest and juice, plus
1 lemon, cut into wedges
2 x 300g packets dwarf green
beans by Sainsbury's, cooked
according to pack instructions

1 Chop the potatoes into large cubes and put them in a large pan of cold water. Bring them to the boil, reduce the heat to a simmer and cook for 20-25 minutes until soft. When they are cooked, drain and mash them with the butter and black pepper until smooth, but still quite dry and stiff.

2 Meanwhile, heat the olive oil in a frying pan and gently cook the leek for 5 minutes until softened, but not browned. Work it into the potato. Set aside, covered, to cool completely.

3 At the same time, bring a large saucepan of water to the boil, then add the smoked haddock and reduce the heat to a simmer. Cook gently for 5-7 minutes (depending on thickness), until the fish flakes easily with a fork. Drain the fish and, when it is cool enough to handle, break it into large flakes with your fingers, removing any bones at the same time. Set aside, covered, to cool completely.

4 Once the potato and fish have cooled, combine them in a large bowl and add the parsley, lemon zest and capers. Mix well, being careful not to break up the fish too much, and check for seasoning. Shape the mixture into 8 fish cakes, cover and rest for 10 minutes in the fridge.

5 Prepare 3 shallow bowls, the first with the flour, seasoned with black pepper, the next with the egg and the last with the breadcrumbs. Dip the fish cakes in the flour, patting off any excess, then in the egg, then in the breadcrumbs, being sure they are well coated.

6 Heat a large frying pan and add enough sunflower oil to cover the base of the pan. Fry the fish cakes in batches over a medium heat for 4-5 minutes on each side until crisp, golden, and cooked through.

7 Meanwhile, combine the mayonnaise, capers, parsley and lemon juice and zest to make a tartare sauce. Serve the cooked fish cakes with the sauce, green beans and lemon wedges.

**Per serving** 2308kJ/550kcal (28%), 20.3g fat (29%), 5.7g saturates (29%), 7.3g sugars (8%), 2.19g salt (37%)

**SERVES** 4
**PREP** 15-20 minutes
**COOK** 15 minutes

# Moules marinière

This classic French recipe - mussels in wine, garlic and herbs - translates as 'in the fisherman's style'

3.5kg mussels, from Sainsbury's fish counter
30g sunflower spread
2 onions, finely chopped
2 garlic cloves, crushed
300ml dry white wine
4 bay leaves
2 sprigs of thyme, washed
freshly ground black pepper
4 tbsp chopped flat-leaf parsley, washed

**1** Before you start cooking, prepare the mussels. Scrub the mussels well in cold water, removing beards and any barnacles. Discard any with broken shells or any that do not close tight when tapped on a hard surface.

**2** Melt the sunflower spread in a large, heavy-based saucepan, add the onions, and fry gently until lightly browned. Add the mussels, garlic, wine, bay leaves, thyme and 300ml water. Season with black pepper. Cover, bring to the boil and cook for 5-6 minutes, or until the mussels have opened, shaking frequently.

**3** Remove the mussels with a slotted spoon, discarding any that remain closed. Transfer them to warm bowls, cover and keep warm.

**4** Strain the cooking liquid into a pan and bring to the boil. Add parsley, pour over the mussels and serve at once.

**Per serving** 1144kJ/272kcal (14%), 9.4g fat (13%), 2.1g saturates (11%), 4.8g sugars (5%), 2.02g salt (34%)

# Seafood tempura

Unusually, a good tempura batter should have small lumps.
Use any white fish and a selection of seafood

**FOR THE BATTER**
400ml cold sparkling water
1 egg, beaten
60g cornflour
225g self-raising flour

**FOR THE SEAFOOD**
500ml oil, for deep-frying
175g white fish fillet, such as
plaice, sea bass or salmon, from
Sainsbury's fish counter,
pinboned, skinned and cut
into 2cm strips

115g frozen raw king prawns by
Sainsbury's, defrosted and
patted dry with kitchen paper
8 scallops by Sainsbury's
300g pack Taste the Difference
frozen squid rings by
Sainsbury's, defrosted and
patted dry with kitchen paper

**FOR THE TERIYAKI
DIPPING SAUCE**
1-2 tbsp soy sauce reduced
salt by Sainsbury's
1 tbsp clear honey
2.5cm piece fresh root ginger,
peeled and grated
1 tbsp mirin or dry sherry
1 spring onion, finely sliced

**1** To make the batter, put the water into a large bowl, add the egg and flours and whisk together to form a batter with lots of fine lumps. Cover and refrigerate for 20-30 minutes.

**2** In a small bowl, mix together the ingredients for the teriyaki dipping sauce. Cover and set aside.

**3** Heat the oil in a deep, heavy-based pan to 180°C. Dip the prepared fish, shellfish and squid in the batter, and fry a few pieces at a time until crisp. Ensure that the food is fully submerged in the oil. The batter should remain quite pale in colour. Lift onto kitchen paper and keep warm while you fry the rest. Serve with the dipping sauce.

**Per serving** 2771kJ/661kcal (33%), 30.4g fat (43%), 3.2g saturates (16%), 6g sugars (7%), 1.8g salt (30%)

# Seafood linguine

A traditional Italian dish with a hint of spice and the freshest seafood

500g mussels from Sainsbury's fish counter
2 tbsp olive oil
1 small onion, finely chopped
2 garlic cloves, grated or finely chopped
390g carton chopped tomatoes with basil and oregano by Sainsbury's
1 tbsp tomato purée mixed with 110ml boiling water

¼ tsp chilli flakes
450g baby squid, gutted, cleaned and cut into rings, from Sainsbury's fish counter or Taste the Difference frozen squid rings by Sainsbury's, defrosted and patted dry with kitchen paper
4 tbsp dry white wine
½ lemon, sliced
450g linguine

12 frozen raw jumbo king prawns by Sainsbury's, defrosted and patted dry with kitchen paper
3 tbsp chopped flat-leaf parsley, washed
freshly ground black pepper

1  Before you start cooking, prepare the mussels. Scrub the mussels well in cold water, removing beards and any barnacles. Discard any with broken shells or any that do not close tight when tapped on a hard surface.

2  Heat the oil in a large saucepan and fry the onion and garlic over a low heat, stirring, for 3-4 minutes, or until softened. Add the tomatoes, purée liquid and chilli, then simmer for 1 minute.

3  Place the mussels and squid in a large pan with the wine and lemon, cover and bring to the boil. Cook for 3-4 minutes, or until the mussel shells have opened, shaking. Strain the liquid through a fine sieve and reserve. Discard the lemon and any unopened mussels. Remove most of the mussels from their shells, leaving a few in their shells, to garnish.

4  Cook the linguine according to the pack instructions.

5  Meanwhile, add the mussel cooking liquid to the sauce and simmer, uncovered, for 2-3 minutes, or until slightly reduced. Add the prawns and simmer for 3-4 minutes until the prawns are pink and cooked through. Add the mussels, squid and parsley and season with black pepper.

6  Drain the pasta, return to the pan and toss in the sauce. Tip into a bowl, place the reserved mussels in their shells on top and serve.

**Per serving** 2708kJ/641kcal (32%), 10.3g fat (15%), 2.1g saturates (11%), 10.7g sugars (12%), 1.45g salt (24%)

### Get ahead
The tomato sauce in step 2 can be made up to 2 days in advance, covered and refrigerated. Return to a simmer before continuing.

# Penne with tuna and roasted onion

Easy to prepare using simple ingredients, this pasta dish
is an ideal mid-week meal

3 red onions, cut into wedges
200g cherry tomatoes
few sprigs of thyme
2 tbsp olive oil
2 tuna steaks, about 175g each,
from Sainsbury's fish counter
350g penne

½ lemon, grated zest
pinch of chilli flakes
freshly ground black pepper
½ tbsp balsamic vinegar by
Sainsbury's (optional), to serve

1 Preheat the oven to 200°C/180°C fan/gas 6. Place the onions, tomatoes and thyme in
a large roasting tin, drizzle with 1 tablespoon of the olive oil, then mix well with your hands.
Roast for 15 minutes, or until soft and lightly coloured.

2 Meanwhile, heat a frying pan or griddle until hot. Rub the tuna steaks with the remaining
oil and season. Fry for 3–4 minutes on each side, until the fish is cooked through and flakes
easily. Remove and put to one side, covered, to rest.

3 Cook the pasta in a pan of boiling water for 10 minutes, or until it is cooked, but still has
a bit of bite to it. Drain, reserving a little of the cooking water in the pan. Return the pasta
to the pan and toss together with the roasted onions and tomatoes.

4 Cut the tuna into chunks, add to the pan with the lemon zest and chilli flakes and toss
gently. Season with black pepper, then drizzle with balsamic vinegar (if using), and serve.

**Per serving** 2301kJ/544kcal (27%), 7.9g fat (11%), 1.6g saturates (8%),
12.1g sugars (13%), 0.11g salt (2%)

### Cook's tip
This recipe uses fresh tuna steaks, but a good store
cupboard back up is to use two 200g tins of tuna steaks
in spring water by Sainsbury's. Drain the fish and add
to the pasta along with the chilli flakes and lemon zest.

# Pan-fried scallops with ginger

A delicious treat with an unusual ginger and chilli twist, this dish can also be made with squid or monkfish

2 tbsp olive oil
500g Charlotte or Anya
potatoes, washed and
thinly sliced
12 south coast king scallops
shell on, about 25g each, from
Sainsbury's fish counter,
shells and roe removed
freshly ground black pepper
1 red chilli, deseeded and
finely chopped
2.5cm piece fresh root ginger,
peeled and grated

½ lemon, juice only
handful of fresh flat-leaf parsley,
washed and finely chopped

**FOR THE ANCHOVY DRESSING**
1 ½ tbsp extra virgin olive oil
½ tbsp white wine vinegar
25g anchovy fillets in olive oil
by Sainsbury's, drained and
finely chopped
pinch of sugar (optional)
freshly ground black pepper

**1** Heat 1 ½ tablespoons of the olive oil in a large non-stick frying pan over a medium-high heat. Add the potatoes, and sauté for 15-20 minutes until golden and cooked through. Drain on kitchen paper, and set aside to keep warm.

**2** Meanwhile, make the anchovy dressing. In a jug, whisk together the extra virgin olive oil, vinegar and anchovies until well combined. Taste, and add a pinch of sugar if it needs it. Season with black pepper.

**3** Pat the scallops dry with kitchen paper, and season with black pepper. Put the remaining olive oil in the frying pan over a high heat. When hot, add the scallops. Sear for about 1 minute then turn them over. Add the chilli and ginger, and squeeze over the lemon juice, being careful as it will spit. Remove the pan from the heat, ensuring that the scallops are cooked through, and sprinkle over the parsley.

**4** Serve immediately with the sautéed potatoes and a drizzle of the anchovy dressing.

**Per serving** 1124kJ/268kcal (13%), 10.9g fat (16%), 1.7g saturates (9%), 2.5g sugars (3%), 1.29g salt (22%)

**Get ahead**
Make the anchovy dressing up to 2 days ahead, cover and refrigerate. Return to room temperature and whisk before use.

# Salmon parcels

Cooking in a parcel or 'en papillote' - in a tightly sealed greaseproof paper parcel - ensures that the fish remains moist during cooking

2 x 240g packs responsibly
sourced Scottish salmon fillets
by Sainsbury's,
about 120g each
olive oil, for greasing
4 tomatoes, sliced
2 lemons, sliced
8 sprigs of tarragon
freshly ground black pepper

**FOR THE BEURRE BLANC**
3 tbsp unsalted butter, cut into
small chunks
1 shallot, finely chopped
1/2 tbsp white wine vinegar
freshly ground black pepper
lemon juice, to taste

1 Cut 8 rounds of greaseproof & non-stick baking paper by Sainsbury's large enough for the salmon fillets to fit on half of the round. Use 2 rounds per fillet to create a double thickness. Lightly grease the top round with olive oil. Repeat with the rest.

2 Preheat the oven to 160°C/140°C fan/gas 3. Divide the tomatoes among the rounds, placing them on one half. Place the salmon on top, then the lemon slices and tarragon. Season with black pepper. Fold up the paper to enclose the fish. Crimp the edges to create a tight seal. Place on a baking tray and bake for 15 minutes.

3 Meanwhile, make the beurre blanc. Melt 1 tablespoon of the butter in a small saucepan, add the shallot and cook for 2-3 minutes, or until soft. Add 60ml water and the vinegar, bring to the boil and simmer until the liquid has reduced to about 2 tablespoons.

4 Reduce the heat to very low and add the remaining butter, a few pieces at a time, whisking vigorously between each addition. It is important to keep the stock hot, but don't allow it to boil. Once all the butter has been added, the sauce should be creamy and fairly thick. Remove from the heat, season with black pepper and add lemon juice to taste.

5 Place the cooked salmon parcels on warm plates, and serve immediately, drizzled with beurre blanc.

**Per serving** 1466kJ/352kcal (18%), 24.3g fat (35%), 9.4g saturates (47%), 3.2g sugars (4%), 0.35g salt (6%)

Get ahead
The paper cases can be assembled, and stored in the fridge for 2 hours.

# Roasted mackerel with harissa and carrots

Roasting a fish in this way allows it to take on a rich rounded flavour. To check that the mackerel is cooked, slit the fish at the thickest part; the flesh should be opaque

4 mackerel from Sainsbury's fish counter, gutted, heads removed and washed
4 tsp harissa paste by Sainsbury's
1 ½ tbsp olive oil

500g Chantenay carrots, topped and tailed
400g tin chickpeas, drained and rinsed
1 tbsp dried thyme
1 tbsp cumin seeds

2 limes, quartered
bunch of fresh coriander, washed and finely chopped
2 x 100g bags watercress, spinach and rocket salad by Sainsbury's, to serve

1 Preheat the oven to 200°C/180°C fan/gas 6. Place the mackerel in a roasting tin. Mix the harissa paste and half the oil together. Drizzle the harissa mixture over the fish, making sure they are covered inside and out. Cover and refrigerate for 10 minutes.

2 Meanwhile, toss the carrots with the remaining oil in a roasting tin and cook for 10 minutes. Remove from the oven and add the chickpeas, thyme, cumin seeds and lime wedges, and toss well.

3 Lay the prepared mackerel on top of the vegetables and bake for 20 minutes, or until the carrots are cooked and the fish is cooked through and flakes easily. Scatter with the coriander leaves and serve with the green salad.

**Per serving** 1767kJ/424kcal (21%), 24.5g fat (35%), 4.3g saturates (22%), 8.0g sugars (9%), 0.47g salt (8%)

**Why not try?**
Try making this with potatoes in place of the carrots. Use **1.1kg salad potatoes**, scrubbed and halved, instead of the carrots. Place in the roasting tin with the lime wedges, and toss in olive oil. Lay the prepared fish on top. Roast in the oven for 20–30 minutes, or until the potatoes are cooked and the fish is cooked through and flakes easily. Serve as before.

# Salmon with mushrooms and pak choi

Chestnut mushrooms have a lovely taste and give depth to the mild flavours of salmon and pak choi in this dish

1 tbsp olive oil

1 tbsp soy sauce reduced salt by Sainsbury's

½ tbsp mirin or rice vinegar

5cm piece of fresh root ginger, peeled and finely chopped

2 garlic cloves, grated or finely chopped

freshly ground black pepper

2 x 240g packs Scottish salmon fillets by Sainsbury's

200g pack pak choi, quartered lengthways

250g pack chestnut mushrooms, large ones halved

**1** Preheat the oven to 200°C/180°C fan/gas 6. Put the oil, soy sauce, mirin or rice vinegar, ginger and garlic in a bowl and mix together well. Season with black pepper.

**2** Put the salmon fillets, pak choi and mushrooms in a roasting tin, then drizzle over the oil mixture and combine well. Cover with foil and bake for 10 minutes. Uncover, spoon the juices over the fish and continue to bake for a further 10–15 minutes, or until the salmon is cooked through and flakes easily.

**Per serving** 1362kJ/327kcal (16%), 20.6g fat (29%), 3.1g saturates (16%), 2.2g sugars (2%), 0.51g salt (9%)

### Why not try?

Try making quick stir-fried fish with pak choi. Dice **600g salmon fillets** or chunky white fish. Slice **250g mushrooms** and thickly shred **2 heads of pak choi**. Heat **1 tbsp oil** in large saucepan over a medium heat. Stir-fry the fish and mushrooms for 2 mins. Add the pak choi and stir-fry until slightly wilted and the fish is cooked through and flakes easily. Add the flavourings as in the original recipe but also add ½ **tsp Chinese five-spice powder**. Stir-fry briefly to combine. Moisten with a splash of water, then serve with **egg noodles**.

# Risotto with mussels

Mussels make a lovely risotto; the fennel adds a subtle aniseed flavour to the creamy rice

1kg mussels, from
Sainsbury's fish counter
1 tbsp olive oil
25g unsalted butter
1 onion, finely chopped
freshly ground black pepper
3 garlic cloves, finely chopped
pinch of dried chilli flakes
1 fennel bulb, trimmed and
finely chopped
300g arborio rice by Sainsbury's
120ml white wine

900ml vegetable stock
(made with 1 stock cube
and boiling water)
bunch of fresh flat-leaf parsley,
washed and finely chopped
a few sprigs of dill, washed
and finely chopped
1 lemon, juice only,
to serve (optional)

1 Before you start cooking, prepare the mussels. Scrub the mussels well in cold water, removing beards and any barnacles. Discard any with broken shells or any that do not close tight when tapped on a hard surface.

2 Heat the oil and butter in a heavy-based pan over a medium heat, add the onion and cook for 3-4 minutes until soft. Season with black pepper, stir in the garlic and chilli flakes and cook for 1 minute.

3 Add the fennel, and cook for about 5 minutes until soft, then stir through the rice. Increase the heat, add the wine and let it simmer for 1-2 minutes until it has been absorbed. In a separate saucepan, simmer the stock. Add a ladleful to the rice and stir, until it has been absorbed. Continue doing this for 30-40 minutes, or until the rice is cooked al dente and is creamy. You may not need all the stock or you may need a little more.

4 Stir in the mussels, cover and leave for a few minutes until the mussels have opened (discard any that do not open). Stir through the parsley and dill, and add a squeeze of lemon juice (if using). Taste and season with some black pepper if needed. Serve immediately.

**Per serving** 1175kJ/279kcal (14%), 6.7g fat (10%), 3.0g saturates (15%), 3.1g sugars (3%), 1.64g salt (27%)

SERVES 4
PREP 25 minutes
COOK 30 minutes

# Sea bass with black bean sauce

A wonderful combination. The sea bass combines well with the sauce to create an interesting taste

3 tbsp black beans from 230g carton, SO Organic by Sainsbury's, drained and rinsed
2 tbsp sunflower oil
2 spring onions, finely chopped
5cm piece fresh root ginger, cut into matchsticks
1 garlic clove, very finely sliced
3 tbsp soy sauce reduced salt by Sainsbury's

2 tbsp rice wine or dry sherry
1 tsp caster sugar
300ml fish stock (made with ½ stock cube and boiling water)
1 tsp cornflour
4 sea bass fillets, about 100g each, from Sainsbury's fish counter

**TO SERVE**
sprigs of coriander, washed
2 tsp sesame oil
240g basmati rice, cooked according to pack instructions

1 Heat the oil in a large frying pan over a low heat. Add the spring onions and ginger, and fry over a low heat until aromatic. Add the garlic and stir-fry for another minute.

2 Remove from the heat and add the soy sauce, rice wine or sherry, sugar and three-quarters of the stock. Return to the heat, bring to the boil and simmer for 2-3 minutes. Mix the cornflour with the remaining stock in a small bowl.

3 Arrange the fish on a steamer and cook for 7-8 minutes, covered, over a large saucepan of simmering water, until the fish is cooked through and flakes easily.

4 Meanwhile, stir the cornflour mixture into the hot stock with the beans, stir up to the boil and simmer for 2-3 minutes until thickened slightly.

5 Arrange the fish on a platter with the coriander. Spoon the sauce over and drizzle with sesame oil. Serve with rice.

**Per serving** 1995kJ/475 kcal (24%), 16.7g fat (24%), 3.2g saturates (16%), 3g sugars (3%), 1.43g salt (24%)

**Get ahead**
The black bean sauce can be made up to a day ahead, covered and refrigerated when cool. Return to a simmer before continuing. Add a splash of water, until the consistency is as you prefer.

# Salmon and sweet potato pie

A new take on a classic recipe

4 salmon fillets (about 450g in total), skinned, from Sainsbury's fish counter

750g sweet potatoes, peeled and sliced

25g sunflower spread

1 tbsp plain flour

500ml semi-skimmed milk

freshly ground black pepper

75g frozen or fresh peas

1 bunch of fresh chives, snipped

**1** Preheat the oven to 200°C/180°C fan/gas 6. Put the salmon in a roasting dish and cook for 10–15 minutes, or until it flakes easily. Don't let it dry out too much. Meanwhile, boil the sweet potatoes in a pan of water for 10–15 minutes until soft when pierced with a knife. Drain and mash using a potato masher.

**2** Next, make the sauce. Melt the sunflower spread in a pan, remove from the heat and stir in the flour. Add a little of the milk and stir with a wooden spoon until smooth. Put the pan back on the heat, and gradually add the remaining milk, stirring all the time. Cook, stirring, until it thickens into a smooth sauce. Season with black pepper. Stir the peas and chives into the sauce.

**3** Put the cooked fish in an ovenproof dish and flake it slightly. Pour or spoon the sauce over it, then mix gently to combine. Top with the sweet potato mash, patterning the surface with the back of a fork. Put the pie in the oven to cook for about 30 minutes, or until golden.

**Per serving** 2216kJ/528kcal (26%), 19.3g fat (28%), 5.7g saturates (29%), 17.9g sugars (20%), 0.77g salt (13%)

# Spicy, saucy monkfish

Perfect for a cold winter's night, the delicious blend of spices brings warmth to this dish

1 tbsp vegetable oil
2 onions, finely sliced
2 tbsp paprika
300ml fish stock (made with
½ stock cube and boiling water)
2 x 390g cartons
chopped tomatoes
6 garlic cloves, grated or
finely chopped
4 bay leaves
2 celery sticks, finely sliced
2 carrots, finely sliced

freshly ground black pepper
750g monkfish fillets, skinned
and cut into 2.5cm cubes, from
Sainsbury's fish counter

**FOR THE SPICY SAUCE**
25g sunflower spread
by Sainsbury's
1 onion, finely chopped
1 apple, peeled, cored
and diced
1 tsp ground cumin

1 tsp ground coriander
½ tsp ground ginger
½ tsp ground cloves
¼ tsp cayenne pepper,
or ½ tsp chilli flakes
½ tbsp cornflour
200ml coconut milk light
150ml fish stock (made
with ½ stock cube and
boiling water)

**1** For the sauce, melt the sunflower spread in a saucepan. Add the onion and apple and cook gently for 3-5 minutes until soft. Add the spices and stir for 2-3 minutes. Blend the cornflour to a paste with 2-3 tablespoons of the coconut milk.

**2** Add the remaining coconut milk and the stock to the saucepan and bring to the boil. Stir in the cornflour paste; the sauce will thicken. Cover and set aside.

**3** Heat the oil in a flameproof casserole. Add the onions and cook for 3-5 minutes until soft. Add the paprika, stock, tomatoes, garlic, bay leaves, celery and carrots. Season with black pepper and bring to the boil. Reduce the heat and simmer to reduce by one-third.

**4** Add the sauce and return to the boil. Add the fish. Cover and simmer for 12-15 minutes, or until the fish is cooked through and flakes easily. Discard the bay leaves and serve in warm bowls.

**Per serving** 1510kJ/359kcal (18%), 12.1g fat (17%), 4.5g saturates (23%), 19.2g sugars (21%), 1.67g salt (28%)

### Get ahead
Make the spicy sauce and the stew base up to 2 days ahead, mix, cover and refrigerate. Return to the boil before adding the fish.

# Meat

# Poultry

## Beef

## Lamb

# Pork

# Garlic and chilli chicken with honeyed sweet potatoes

A simple one-pot dish. Sweet potatoes can break up easily, so be sure that they don't cook for too long

850g pack British chicken
thighs and drumsticks
by Sainsbury's
freshly ground black pepper
4 sweet potatoes, peeled and
cut into big chunks
2 tbsp clear honey
1 tbsp extra virgin olive oil

2 red chillies, deseeded
and diced
a few sprigs of thyme
3 garlic cloves, crushed
125ml dry white wine
300ml chicken stock (made with
1/2 stock cube and boiling water)

1 Preheat the oven to 200°C/180°C fan/gas 6. Season the chicken with black pepper, and coat the sweet potatoes in the honey.

2 In a non-stick frying pan, heat 1/2 tablespoon of the oil over a medium heat. Add the chicken pieces and cook for about 5 minutes on each side, until golden all over. Transfer to an ovenproof dish, cover and set aside.

3 Heat the remaining oil in the same frying pan. Add the sweet potatoes and cook, stirring, for about 5 minutes, until beginning to colour; the honey should caramelize but not burn. Add the chillies, thyme and garlic, season with black pepper and add to the chicken.

4 Pour in the wine and stock, cover the casserole and transfer to the oven to cook for 40 minutes. Check the casserole a few times during cooking; give it a stir if needed, or add a small amount of stock if it is too dry. To check that the chicken is cooked, pierce the joints with a skewer; the juices should run clear and there should be no pink remaining. Serve hot.

**Per serving** 2307kJ/549kcal (28%), 20.4g fat (29%), 5.3g saturates (27%), 13.5g sugars (15%), 0.94g salt (16%)

# Pot-roasted guinea fowl

In this dish, the slow braising of the guinea fowl allows the tender cabbage to soak up the rich flavours of the stock, transforming the Savoy cabbage into something special

2 guinea fowl, about 1kg each
freshly ground black pepper
30g unsalted butter
1 tbsp extra virgin olive oil
1 small onion, finely chopped
1 leek, thinly sliced
2 celery sticks, sliced
100g bacon lardons
by Sainsbury's

85g walnuts, halved
1 small Savoy cabbage,
about 400g
100ml hot chicken stock
(made with $1/2$ reduced salt
stock cube and boiling water)

1 Preheat the oven to 200°C/180°C fan/gas 6. Season the guinea fowls with black pepper.

2 Heat the butter with half the oil in a large, deep, flameproof casserole, and fry the guinea fowl on a medium heat for 10 minutes, turning to colour on all sides. Remove from the heat, lift out the birds, cover and set aside.

3 Add the remaining oil to the casserole with the onion, leek, celery and lardons, and fry, stirring, for 2–3 minutes, or until lightly coloured. Add the walnuts, then place the guinea fowl back on top of the fried vegetables.

4 Cut the cabbage into 8 wedges. Tuck them into the casserole. Pour over the hot stock. Bring to the boil, then cover and cook in the preheated oven for 45 minutes, or until the vegetables are tender and the guinea fowl is piping hot with no pink remaining, and the juices run clear when pierced with a skewer.

5 Leave to stand for 10 minutes before serving. To serve, remove the guinea fowl from the casserole, arrange on a serving plate and serve with vegetables and stock.

**Per serving** 3687kJ/885kcal (44%), 58.3g fat (83%), 12.3g saturates (6.2%), 7.7g sugars (9%), 2.13g salt (36%)

# Chicken pie with mushrooms, leeks and bacon

This creamy chicken pie has the additional flavours of earthy mushrooms and sweet leeks to create a delicious family meal

**FOR THE FILLING**
100g pancetta, diced
1 onion, finely chopped
2 leeks, about 200g, cut into 1cm slices
150g closed cup mushrooms, wiped and halved or quartered, if necessary
460g pack Sainsbury's British chicken breast fillets, cut into 2.5cm chunks

1 heaped tbsp chopped thyme
1 heaped tbsp chopped flat-leaf parsley
1 tbsp plain flour
300ml semi-skimmed milk
1 tbsp Dijon mustard
freshly ground black pepper

**FOR THE PASTRY**
250g ready rolled light puff pastry by Sainsbury's
plain flour, for dusting
1 egg, beaten, for glazing

**TO SERVE**
2 x 200g packs Tenderstem broccoli by Sainsbury's

1 Preheat the oven to 200°C/180°C fan/gas 6. Cook the pancetta in a large saucepan until it releases some fat. Add the onion and fry for 5 minutes until softened and pale golden. Add the leeks and mushrooms and cook for a further 3-5 minutes until the pancetta is crisp. Transfer to a plate, cover and set aside.

2 Add the chicken and herbs to the same pan. Fry over a high heat for 3-4 minutes until coloured on all sides. Return the leeks, mushrooms and pancetta to the pan. Sprinkle the flour over the pie filling and stir it in well. Pour over the milk, add the mustard and black pepper and bring to the boil, stirring constantly. The mixture should thicken as it heats. Reduce the heat to low and cook for a further 5 minutes until the liquid has reduced and the chicken is cooked through with no pink remaining. Transfer the filling to an 18cm pie dish.

3 Cut the pastry into a round bigger than the pie dish. Cut the leftover pastry into long strips. Brush the rim of the dish with a little of the beaten egg and press the pastry strips around the rim. Brush the edging with more beaten egg and top with the pastry lid. Press down to seal the lid, then trim away any excess pastry. Use any pastry trimmings to decorate the pie.

4 Brush the top of the pie with beaten egg, then cut two slits in the top to allow steam to escape. Bake for 20-25 minutes until golden. Set aside to rest for 5 minutes before serving. Cook the broccoli according to the pack instructions, and serve alongside the pie.

**Per serving** 2456kJ/585kcal (29%), 23.3g fat (33%), 9g saturates (45%), 9.8g sugars (11%), 0.92g salt (15%)

# Chicken, butternut squash and saffron with wild rice

This aromatic and colourful dish will brighten a winter evening

460g pack British chicken
breast fillets by Sainsbury's,
cut into bite-sized pieces
1 tbsp olive oil
freshly ground black pepper
1 onion, roughly chopped
75g reduced salt back bacon,
chopped into bite-sized pieces
2 tbsp plain flour

2 carrots, peeled and
roughly chopped
6 garlic cloves, unpeeled
900ml Signature chicken
stock by Sainbury's
1 bay leaf
300g butternut squash,
peeled, deseeded and cut
into bite-sized chunks

1 orange, zest and juice
pinch of saffron threads
240g basmati and wild rice
by Sainsbury's
handful of fresh parsley,
washed and chopped, to serve

1 Preheat the oven to 200ºC/180ºC fan/gas 6. Rub the chicken with the oil and season well with black pepper. Heat a large, flameproof casserole and add the chicken. Cook for about 4 minutes, turning occasionally. Add the onion and bacon and continue to sauté until the chicken and onion are golden. Stir in the flour and scrape up all the pan juices. Cook for 1 minute, stirring.

2 Add the carrots, whole garlic cloves and a little of the stock. Bring to the boil and stir, then pour in the remaining stock. Add the bay leaf, butternut squash, orange zest and juice and saffron. Season with black pepper and stir. Transfer the casserole to the oven and cook for 40 minutes, topping it up with hot water if the mixture becomes too dry.

3 Meanwhile, cook the rice according to the pack instructions. Drain and keep warm. Remove the garlic cloves from the casserole with a slotted spoon, and then squeeze them out of their skins and put back into the casserole.

4 Divide the rice between 4 bowls or plates and ladle over the chicken and butternut squash mixture. Scatter with the parsley to serve.

**Per serving** 2234kJ/529kcal (27%), 9g fat (13%), 2.3g saturates (12%), 10.7g sugars (12%), 2.36g salt (39%)

# Turkey kebabs

These delicious turkey kebabs are low in fat. Serve with a refreshing mint yogurt

60ml reduced salt soy sauce by Sainsbury's

1 tbsp olive oil

2 garlic cloves, finely chopped

3/4 tsp ground ginger

1/4 tsp chilli flakes

3 x 260g packs British turkey breast fillets by Sainsbury's, cut into 2.5cm cubes

1 red pepper, deseeded and cut into 2.5cm pieces

1 yellow pepper, deseeded and cut into 2.5cm pieces

1 large courgette, cut into 2.5cm slices

240ml low-fat natural yogurt

2 tbsp mint, washed and chopped

1/2 tsp ground cumin

2 x 120g bags bistro salad by Sainsbury's, to serve

1 Combine the soy sauce, oil, garlic, ginger and chilli. Add the turkey pieces and toss to coat. Cover, chill and marinate for at least 1 hour in the fridge.

2 Thread the turkey, peppers and courgette onto skewers and brush with any leftover marinade. Grill for 5-6 minutes on each side, or until cooked through with no pink remaining.

3 Mix together the yogurt, mint and cumin in a small bowl. Arrange the kebabs on a serving platter with the mint yogurt and green salad on the side.

**Per serving** 736kJ/175kcal (9%), 3.8g fat (5%), 1.3%g saturates (7%), 7.9g sugars (9%), 1.21g salt (20%)

### Cook's tip
If using wooden skewers, soak them in cold water for 30 minutes before using to prevent them from burning.

# Quick turkey cassoulet

A great way to use leftover roast turkey (see p114) to make a family meal. A breadcrumb crust adds wholemeal crunch to the savoury filling

1½ tbsp olive oil

1 medium red onion, finely chopped

2 garlic cloves, crushed

1 red pepper, deseeded and diced

60g Be good to yourself smoked bacon medallions by Sainsbury's, roughly chopped

2 celery sticks, finely chopped

390g carton chopped tomatoes

250ml chicken stock (made with ½ stock cube and boiling water)

2 tsp soy sauce reduced salt by Sainsbury's

75g wholemeal breadcrumbs

30g Parmesan cheese, grated

3 tbsp chopped flat-leaf parsley

2 tsp Dijon mustard

2 x 400g tins mixed pulses by Sainsbury's, drained and rinsed

400g cooked turkey meat, roughly chopped

**1** Heat 1 tablespoon of the oil in a large non-stick saucepan, add the onion and cook over a low heat for 5 minutes. Add the garlic, red pepper, bacon and celery and cook for a further 5 minutes, stirring occasionally.

**2** Add the tomatoes, stock and soy sauce. Bring to the boil, then reduce to a fast simmer and cook for 15 minutes, or until the sauce begins to thicken.

**3** Meanwhile, mix together the breadcrumbs, Parmesan and parsley.

**4** Add the mustard, beans and turkey to the saucepan and cook for a further 5-7 minutes until the turkey is heated through thoroughly.

**5** Transfer the hot mixture into a shallow ovenproof dish. Sprinkle the breadcrumb mixture evenly over the top and drizzle over the remaining olive oil. Place under a medium-hot grill for 5 minutes, or until the top is golden, then serve immediately.

**Per serving** 998kJ/238kcal (12%), 6.6g fat (9%), 1.9g saturates (10%), 6.3g sugars (7%), 1.52g salt (25%)

# Mustard chicken casserole

Chicken and mustard is a classic combination. If you have the time, let the chicken marinate for a few hours

2 tbsp wholegrain mustard by Sainsbury's
1 tbsp English mustard
2 tbsp runny honey
1.3kg pack British chicken thighs by Sainsbury's
freshly ground black pepper
1 tbsp olive oil

2 onions, roughly chopped
2 tbsp plain flour
300g parsnips, peeled and roughly chopped
a few sprigs of thyme
900ml vegetable or chicken stock (made using 1 stock cube and boiling water)

450g leeks washed, trimmed, cut in half lengthways, and finely sliced, to serve

**1** Preheat the oven to 160°C/140°C fan/gas 3. Mix together the mustards in a bowl and stir through the honey. Season the chicken thighs with black pepper, then smother them with the mustard mixture. Cover and leave to marinate in the fridge for 30 minutes, or longer if time permits.

**2** Heat half the oil in a large flameproof casserole over a medium-high heat and add the chicken pieces, a few at a time. Cook for 6-10 minutes until golden - be careful, as the honey may cause them to colour quickly. Remove, cover and set aside.

**3** Heat the remaining oil in the casserole over a medium heat, add the onions and toss them around the casserole to coat in any juices. Add the flour and stir to scrape up the sticky bits from the bottom, then add the parsnips and thyme. Pour in the stock, bring to the boil and then reduce to a simmer. Return the chicken to the casserole together with any juices, nestling them in between the parsnips and making sure they are covered in liquid. Cover and put in the oven for 1 hour 30 minutes. Check occasionally that it's not drying out, topping up with a little hot water if needed.

**4** Meanwhile, arrange the leeks in a steamer over a pan of boiling water, reduce the heat and steam for 8-10 minutes until the leeks are tender and piping hot. Once the casserole is cooked, remove it from the oven, taste and season with black pepper. Serve with the hot steamed leeks.

**Per serving** 1593kJ/381kcal (19%), 19.0g fat (27%), 4.8g saturates (24%), 13.4g sugars (15%), 1.28g salt (21%)

# Turkey and pesto meatballs

Pesto, with its fresh basil and olive oil, adds another layer of flavour to these moist meatballs

500g turkey breast mince 2% fat by Sainsbury's
150g breadcrumbs made from day-old white farmhouse loaf
1 egg
1 shallot, finely chopped
360g dried penne pasta

FOR THE PESTO
50g pine nuts
60g fresh basil leaves
3 garlic cloves
50g freshly grated Parmesan, plus a little extra for sprinkling
freshly ground black pepper
50ml extra virgin olive oil

1 In a dry frying pan, lightly toast the pine nuts for 2-3 minutes, or until golden, and set aside to cool. In a food processor or using a hand blender, combine the basil, garlic, Parmesan, pine nuts and black pepper. Pulse to combine. Turn the processor on high and add 2-3 tablespoons of the oil in a thin drizzle, and process to a thick paste.

2 Preheat the oven to 180ºC/160ºC fan/gas 4. Line a baking tray with greaseproof & non-stick baking paper by Sainsbury's. In a large bowl, combine the turkey, breadcrumbs, egg, black pepper, shallot and half of the pesto. Stir well to incorporate.

3 Form the turkey mixture into evenly sized balls, approximately 5cm in diameter. Place on the lined baking tray. Bake for 30-40 minutes, or until the meatballs turn golden.

4 Meanwhile, cook the pasta according to the pack instructions. Drain and toss in the remaining pesto along with the remaining oil and the meatballs. Serve hot, sprinkled with grated Parmesan.

**Per serving** 3534kJ/840kcal (42%), 25.3g fat (36%), 5.2g saturates (26%), 6g sugars (7%), 0.81g salt (14%)

### Why not try?
Make beef meatballs by combining a **500g pack beef mince 5% fat by Sainsbury's**, 2 eggs, 60g freshly grated Parmesan, 150g breadcrumbs and **2 teaspoons each of dried oregano, basil, thyme** and **rosemary**. Form the mixture into evenly sized balls, and bake as above. Serve the meatballs with **tomato and jalapeño relish by Sainsbury's**.

# Chicken tikka masala

A British favourite, this creamy, delicately spiced curry is believed to have originated in Glasgow

460g pack British chicken breast fillets by Sainsbury's, cut into bite-sized chunks
1/2 tsp chilli powder
1 tbsp lemon juice
100ml low-fat natural yogurt
5cm piece of fresh root ginger, peeled and grated
4 tsp garam masala
2 tbsp sunflower oil

2 onions, thinly sliced
3 garlic cloves, finely chopped
1 tsp paprika
240g basmati rice
390g carton chopped tomatoes by Sainsbury's
200ml chicken stock (made with 1/2 stock cube and boiling water)
3 tbsp single cream

**TO SERVE**
28g pack fresh coriander by Sainsbury's, washed and chopped
2 limes, cut into wedges

1 Place the chicken pieces in a bowl. Add the chilli powder, lemon juice, yogurt, half the ginger and 1 teaspoon of garam masala, and mix well. Cover and place in the fridge for at least 1 hour, or overnight.

2 If using wooden skewers, soak them in the water for at least 30 minutes before using. Preheat the grill to high. Thread the chicken on to the skewers and place on a baking tray. Grill for 5 minutes on each side until golden and cooked through, with no pink remaining. Remove the chicken from the skewers.

3 Meanwhile, heat the oil in a large pan and fry the onions over a medium heat for 10 minutes until golden. Stir in the garlic and remaining ginger, and cook for 1 further minute. Stir in the paprika and the remaining 3 teaspoons of garam masala, and fry for about 1 minute until the spices release their aromas. In the meantime, cook the rice according to the pack instructions.

4 Pour in the tomatoes and stock, and bring to the boil. Turn down to a low-medium heat, and simmer for 5 minutes until slightly thickened. Stir in the cream and add the chicken pieces. Simmer for 1 further minute, then stir through half the coriander.

5 Garnish the chicken tikka masala with the remaining coriander and serve on a bed of rice, with the lime wedges on the side.

**Per serving** 2252kJ/534kcal (27%), 11.6g fat (17%), 3.2g saturates (16%), 10g sugars (11%), 0.79g salt (13%)

# Chicken stuffed with shiitake mushrooms

Shiitake mushrooms are full of flavour and make a delicious filling for chicken breasts. Serve alongside mashed potato for an easy family supper

50g dried shiitake mushrooms by Sainsbury's
460g pack British chicken breast fillets by Sainsbury's
freshly ground black pepper
handful of fresh thyme sprigs, leaves picked
splash of chilli oil (optional)
1 tbsp olive oil
2 x 200g packs pak choi, heads halved and cooked according to pack instructions, to serve

**FOR THE MASHED POTATOES**
1kg Maris Piper or King Edward potatoes
30ml semi-skimmed milk
25g unsalted butter
freshly ground black pepper

**1** Put the dried mushrooms in a small bowl. Cover with 1 litre boiling water, and leave to soak for 40 minutes. Drain, using a fine sieve to remove any grit, and reserve the soaking liquid. Roughly chop the rehydrated mushrooms, cover and set aside.

**2** Slice the chicken breasts lengthways to form a pocket – be careful not to cut all the way through. Season with black pepper, and scatter with half of the thyme leaves. Put the soaked mushrooms, remaining thyme and chilli oil (if using), in a bowl and season with black pepper. Mix together, then stuff each chicken breast with the mixture, and fold over the top to seal.

**3** Heat the olive oil in a large frying pan over a medium-high heat. Carefully add the chicken, pocket-side down. Leave to cook undisturbed for 6–8 minutes, then turn over and cook the other side for about the same time until cooked through with no pink remaining. Remove from the pan, cover and set aside to keep warm.

**4** While the chicken is cooking, place the potatoes in a large pan, cover with cold water, bring to the boil and cook for 10–15 minutes until tender. Drain and mash with the milk and butter, and season with black pepper.

**5** Add the reserved soaking liquid from the mushrooms to the pan. Increase the heat, and let boil and reduce by half. To serve, spoon a little of the reduced mushroom stock over the chicken, and serve with creamy mashed potato and the pak choi.

**Per serving** 1998kJ/474kcal (24%), 11.7g fat (17%), 4.2g saturates (21%), 3.1g sugars (3%), 0.36g salt (6%)

# Jamaican jerk chicken with mango salsa

Serve this spicy chicken with mango salsa for a taste of the Caribbean

4 spring onions,
roughly chopped

1 garlic clove, chopped

2cm piece fresh root ginger,
peeled and finely chopped

1 red chilli, deseeded and finely
chopped, or more to taste

2 tbsp sunflower oil

2 tbsp soy sauce reduced salt

1 tbsp cider vinegar

1/2 lime, zest and juice

1/2 tsp dried thyme

1/2 tsp ground allspice

1/4 tsp ground nutmeg

1/4 tsp ground cinnamon

1 tbsp soft, dark brown sugar

freshly ground black pepper

1kg pack British chicken
drumsticks by Sainsbury's

**FOR THE MANGO SALSA**

2 ripe, firm mangoes, peeled,
stoned and cut into small cubes

2 tbsp finely chopped mint
leaves, washed

1 red chilli, deseeded and
finely chopped

1 lime, juice only

freshly ground black pepper

2 x 170g bags Italian-style salad
by Sainsbury's, to serve

**1** For the sauce, place all the ingredients except the chicken in a food processor (or in a bowl if using a hand blender). Pulse to a thick, smooth sauce, scraping down the sides with a spatula during the process. Remove and place in a large bowl.

**2** Cut 2 or 3 slashes on each side of the chicken pieces, where the meat is thickest. Add to the sauce, and mix to coat. Cover and marinate in the fridge for at least 2 hours, turning over once halfway through to ensure they are evenly coated.

**3** Preheat the oven to 190°C/170°C fan/gas 5. Roast the chicken for approximately 30 minutes, turning over and basting with the leftover jerk sauce halfway through the cooking time.

**4** The meat will separate slightly where it has been slashed, which enables it to cook right through and gives a bigger surface area for the sauce. The chicken is cooked through if the juices run clear when the meat is pierced at its thickest point with a skewer and no pink remains.

**5** While the chicken is cooking, make the mango salsa. Place all of the salsa ingredients in a bowl and mix well. Season with black pepper and serve with the chicken and green salad.

**Per serving** 1595kJ/381kcal (19%), 17.2g fat (25%), 3.9g saturates (20%), 17.3g sugars (19%), 0.92g salt (15%)

# Devilled chicken

Devilling means serving food in a spicy mix. It is thought that the term was first used in 18th century England

2 tbsp wholegrain mustard
2 tbsp mango chutney by Sainsbury's
2 tbsp Worcestershire sauce
¼ tsp ground paprika
3 tbsp orange juice
1 red chilli, chopped (optional)
2 tbsp olive oil
460g pack British chicken breast fillets by Sainsbury's, beaten thin and cut into strips

1 red onion finely chopped
1 red pepper, cored and cut into strips
1 orange pepper, cored and cut into strips
1 garlic clove, crushed

**TO SERVE**
½ tbsp sunflower oil
260g bag young leaf spinach by Sainsbury's
2 garlic cloves, chopped

1 Mix together the mustard, chutney, Worcestershire sauce, paprika, orange juice and chilli (if using) until well combined.

2 Heat the oil in a frying pan or wok, add the chicken and cook over a high heat until golden. Remove the chicken from the pan and set aside, covered to keep it warm.

3 Add the onion to the pan and fry for 2-3 minutes, or until beginning to colour. Add the peppers and garlic and fry, stirring constantly, for 3-4 minutes, or until tender.

4 Stir in the mustard mixture and return the chicken to the pan. Cook for 5 minutes, or until piping hot and the chicken is cooked through with no pink remaining.

5 For the spinach, heat the sunflower oil in a pan, add the spinach leaves and garlic and stir-fry for 2 minutes until the spinach wilts. Serve immediately with the chicken.

**Per serving** 1415kJ/337kcal (17%), 10.5g fat (15%), 1.7g saturates (9%), 15.2g sugars (17%), 1g salt (17%)

### Cook's tip
To beat the chicken into thin escalopes for cutting into strips, place the fillets between two pieces of cling film and flatten with a meat tenderizer or rolling pin.

SERVES 4
PREP 30 minutes
COOK 1 hour 40 minutes

# Chicken Parmesan

Treat family and friends with this tasty dish infused with the flavours of Italy

650g pack of British chicken breast fillets by Sainsbury's
40g plain flour
1 tsp garlic granules
½ tsp white pepper
40g breadcrumbs made with day-old farmhouse white loaf
50g freshly grated Parmesan, plus 30g extra for the topping
1 egg, beaten with ½–1 tbsp water

1 tbsp olive oil, for frying
125g pack Be good to yourself 10% fat mozzarella cheese by Sainsbury's, cut into slices
2 x 170g bags of Italian-style salad by Sainsbury's, to serve

**FOR THE SAUCE**
½ tbsp olive oil
1 onion, diced
2 garlic cloves, crushed
400g fresh tomatoes, diced

125ml chicken stock (made with ½ stock cube and boiling water)
½ tbsp chopped rosemary
½ tsp chopped basil
½ tsp dried oregano
½ tsp dried thyme
freshly ground black pepper

1 For the sauce, heat the oil in a large saucepan over a medium heat. Add the onion and garlic and cook for 5 minutes, stirring, until caramelized. Add the remaining ingredients, and reduce the heat to a simmer. Cook for 45 minutes, stirring occasionally. Taste and season with black pepper, if necessary.

2 Place the chicken between two pieces of cling film and flatten with a meat tenderizer or rolling pin. Mix the flour and half the seasonings in a shallow dish. Combine the breadcrumbs, Parmesan and remaining seasoning in a second dish. Place the beaten egg in a small bowl. Heat the oil in a heavy-based pan. Dust the chicken with the flour mixture, dip in the beaten egg and coat with the breadcrumb mixture. Fry the chicken for 4 minutes on each side until it is cooked through with no pink remaining.

3 Set the grill to its highest setting. Transfer the sauce to a casserole or low-sided ovenproof dish to fit under the grill and add the chicken, partially covering it with sauce. Top with both lots of cheese and grill for 15 minutes, or until the mozzarella has melted and is bubbling. Serve hot with the green salad.

**Per serving** 2369kJ/564kcal (28%), 19.5g fat (28%), 8.2g saturates (41%), 6.9g sugars (8%), 1.68g salt (28%)

# Spicy honeyed chicken with chilli greens

This is a great way to spice up chicken. Serve with hot, stir-fried greens for an unusual meal

200g pack of 2 pak choi, sliced
½ tbsp soy sauce reduced salt by Sainsbury's
2.5cm piece of fresh root ginger, peeled and grated
pinch of chilli flakes
freshly ground black pepper
2 tbsp clear honey

2 limes, juice only
2 tbsp extra virgin olive oil
1 tsp five-spice powder mixed with 1 tbsp sesame oil
2 x 660g packs Sainsbury's British chicken thighs and drumsticks

1 Preheat the oven to 200°C/180°C fan/gas 6. Put the greens in a large bowl. Add the soy sauce, ginger, chilli flakes and black pepper, and toss to combine. Cover and set aside.

2 In another bowl, mix together the honey, lime juice, ½ tablespoon of the oil and the five-spice paste, until well combined. Spread over the chicken and season with black pepper. Cover and leave to marinate in the fridge for at least 20 minutes.

3 Heat 1 tablespoon of the oil in a large frying pan over a medium-high heat. Add the chicken pieces, skin-side down; cook a few pieces at a time if the pan is not big enough. Cook for 5–8 minutes on each side until golden and crispy, then transfer to a roasting tin. Roast in the oven for about 40 minutes until the chicken is cooked through with no pink remaining and the juices run clear when a joint is pierced with a skewer.

4 Meanwhile, wipe the frying pan with kitchen paper, reduce the heat slightly and add the greens. Drizzle over the remaining ½ tablespoon of oil, and stir-fry for about 5 minutes until beginning to wilt. Serve hot with the chicken.

**Per serving** 1340kJ/320kcal (16%), 16.2g fat (23%), 3.7g saturates (19%), 5.1g sugars (6%), 0.32g salt (5%)

# Herb roasted chicken

Herb butter adds plenty of flavour to this roast and helps keep the chicken moist as it cooks

30g unsalted butter, softened
1 tbsp finely chopped tarragon
1 tbsp finely chopped
flat-leaf parsley
1 tbsp chopped thyme
1 garlic clove, crushed

½ lemon, zest and juice
freshly ground black pepper
2kg British whole large chicken
by Sainsbury's
1 tbsp olive oil

1 Preheat the oven to 200°C/180°C fan/gas 6. For the herb butter, place the butter, herbs, garlic and lemon zest in a large bowl and mash together to combine. Season with black pepper.

2 Place the chicken on a clean work surface. Loosen the skin on the chicken breast and gently separate it from the meat, without tearing the skin, creating a pocket. Spread the herb butter evenly under the skin.

3 Place the chicken in a large roasting tin. Rub the skin with the oil and season. Drizzle over the lemon juice and place the lemon shell in the body cavity.

4 Transfer to the oven and roast for 1 hour 40 minutes, or until piping hot and no pink colour remains: the juices should run clear when a skewer is inserted into the thickest part of the thigh. Rest for 15 minutes, covered with foil, before serving.

**Per serving** 1636kJ/391kcal (20%), 21.7g fat (31%), 7.1g saturates (36%), <0.5g sugars (<1%), 0.21g salt (4%)

## Cook's tip
Try placing the chicken on a roasting rack within a roasting tin to help stop the bottom becoming soggy and greasy, and to help it cook more evenly. If you haven't got a rack then try sitting the chicken on a bed of roughly chopped vegetables.

# Tips for Christmas cooking

The secret to a successful Christmas lunch is all in the timing. Planning ahead is key, and thinking of the roast turkey as a large roast chicken helps! Here is a suggested menu and basic timeline for the big day

## Christmas Menu

### Starter
French onion soup                                              p8

### Main
Roast turkey                                                   p114
or
Vegetable lasagne                                             p194

*with*
Roasted root vegetables                                       p220
Brussels sprouts with chestnuts and pancetta                 p224
Sage and onion stuffing balls                                p236
Roast potatoes                                                p238

### Desserts
Raspberry and white chocolate trifle                         p244
Mince pies                                                    p280

## Plan ahead

**December 23rd**
- Make the **Mince pies**
  Store in airtight container
  Total time: 30-35 minutes, plus chilling

**December 24th**
- Make the **Vegetable lasagne**
  Cool and store covered in the fridge
  Total time: 55 minutes

- Make **French onion soup** up to step 2
  Cool and store covered in the fridge; add croûtes just before serving
  Total time: 1 hour 20 minutes

- Make the **Trifle** up to step 2
  Cool and store covered in the fridge; add whipped cream just before serving
  Total time: 15 minutes

# Christmas day planner

**9.30am**
- Prepare the vegetables for the side dishes
- Prepare the stuffing mixture

**10.00am**
- Preheat the oven to 190°C/170°C fan/gas 5
- Prepare the turkey

**10.30am**
- Put the turkey in the oven, uncovered

**11.00am**
- Cover the turkey loosely with a piece of buttered foil, then return to the oven and roast for 2 hours 30 minutes, basting every 30-45 minutes

**12.15pm**
- Prepare the redcurrant glaze for the turkey

**12.45pm**
- Boil the potatoes

**1.00pm**
- Remove the turkey from the oven and brush all over with the redcurrant glaze. Return to the oven, uncovered, for 30 minutes until cooked
- Put the root vegetables and the potatoes in the oven
- Reheat the **Vegetable lasagne**, if using

**1.15pm**
- Reheat the **French onion soup** and toast the croûtes

**1.30pm**
- Remove the turkey from the oven; the juices should run clear when a skewer is inserted into the thickest part of the thigh. Allow to rest for 30 minutes
- Form the stuffing mixture into balls and put in the oven
- Serve the starters

**1.45pm**
- Cook the **Brussels sprouts with chestnuts and pancetta**

**2.00pm**
- Carve and serve the turkey and the Vegetable lasagne with the stuffing balls and vegetables

**Later...**
- Serve dessert when everyone is ready!

## Turkey tips

Don't waste your turkey giblets - make gravy! Fry the giblets in a large pan with **1 roughly chopped onion**. When brown, add **250ml red wine** to deglaze. Add a few **sprigs of thyme, 1 bay leaf** and **1 litre chicken stock**. Bring to the boil and simmer for about 20 minutes. Strain this through a fine sieve and reduce the gravy by gently simmering on the hob to reach the desired thickness.

# Roast turkey

A roast turkey is great for a family celebration at any time of the year

75g unsalted butter, softened,
plus extra for greasing
handful of fresh rosemary
leaves, chopped
4.8kg Taste the Difference
free-range Norfolk Black turkey
by Sainsbury's, giblets removed,
or 4.55kg frozen whole basted
turkey by Sainsbury's, defrosted
according to pack instructions

1 onion, halved
1 fresh bay leaf
2 tbsp redcurrant jelly
1 tbsp mint sauce
freshly ground black pepper
handful of thyme sprigs, washed

1 Preheat the oven to 190°C/170°C fan/gas 5. In a bowl, mix together the butter and half the rosemary leaves.

2 Use your fingertips to separate the skin from the turkey breast meat. Push the herb butter into this 'pocket' and spread over the breast in an even layer by pressing down on the skin with your hand to smear.

3 Put the onion and bay leaf into the cavity of the turkey, then tie the legs together with kitchen string. Put the turkey in a large roasting tin, breast side up. Roast uncovered for 30 minutes.

4 Remove from the oven and cover loosely with a piece of buttered foil, then return to the oven and roast for a further 2 hours 30 minutes, basting every 30-45 minutes.

5 Meanwhile, put the redcurrant jelly and mint sauce in a pan and heat until the jelly has melted. Stir in the remaining rosemary and set aside. About 30 minutes before the end of the cooking time, remove the turkey and brush all over with the redcurrant glaze. Return to the oven, uncovered, for the final 30 minutes until piping hot and no pink remains: the juices should run clear when a skewer is inserted into the thickest part of the thigh.

6 Transfer the turkey to a warmed serving plate, season, scatter with sprigs of thyme and allow to rest for 30 minutes, covered loosely with foil. Carve and serve.

**Per serving** 1968kJ/469kcal (24%), 21.9g fat (31%), 8.8g saturates (44%), <0.5g sugars (<1%), 0.31g salt (5%)

**Love your leftovers**
Keep leftover turkey covered in the fridge, and use within 48 hours. Make the most of your leftover turkey in soups, curries, or cassoulet (see p92).

# Spicy turkey burgers

These tasty burgers are quick to prepare and make an alternative to the usual beef

500g pack turkey mince
2% fat by Sainsbury's
2 tbsp finely chopped onion
2 tbsp chopped parsley
2 tsp Dijon mustard
2 garlic cloves, finely chopped
60g fresh breadcrumbs
1 egg white
freshly ground black pepper
1 tbsp vegetable oil

TO SERVE
4 SO organic wholemeal
seeded rolls
by Sainsbury's
1 large ripe tomato, sliced
½ red onion, thinly sliced
2 handfuls of shredded lettuce

1 Mix the turkey, onion, parsley, mustard, garlic, breadcrumbs and egg white in a bowl, and season with pepper. Form into 4 equally sized burgers.

2 Heat the oil in a large frying pan. Add the burgers and fry for 4-5 minutes on each side, or until golden and cooked through, with no pink remaining. Meanwhile, split and toast the buns.

3 Place a turkey burger into each bun, with 1-2 tomato slices, sliced red onion and some shredded lettuce.

Per serving 2032kJ/484kcal (24%), 17.0g fat (24%), 3.0g saturates (15%), 5.6g sugars (6%), 1.69g salt (28%)

Get ahead
The turkey burgers can be made a day in advance. Wrap tightly in cling film and chill in the fridge overnight.

# Boeuf bourguignon

A simplified version of a French classic, the beef here is meltingly tender and delicious

2 tbsp olive oil
½ x 200g pack Be good to yourself unsmoked bacon medallions by Sainsbury's, cut into lardons
2 onions, finely chopped
4 thin carrots, cut into chunks

1 celery stick, finely chopped
150g closed cup white mushrooms, halved if large
750g beef braising steak from Sainsbury's meat counter, cut into 3cm cubes
2 tbsp plain flour

freshly ground black pepper
300ml red wine
200ml beef stock (made with ½ stock cube and boiling water)
5g bouquet garni by Sainsbury's

1 Preheat the oven to 150°C/130°C fan/gas 2. Heat 1 tablespoon of the oil in a large flameproof casserole. Fry the lardons for a few minutes until lightly coloured. Add the onions, carrots, celery and mushrooms, and cook for 5 minutes. Cover and set aside.

2 Pat the beef dry with kitchen paper. Season the flour with black pepper and toss the beef in it to coat. Shake off the excess.

3 Heat the remaining oil in the pan and fry the beef, in batches, until coloured on all sides. Cover and set aside.

4 Pour the wine and stock into the pan, stirring to dislodge any meaty residue. Season with black pepper, add the bouquet garni and return the meat and vegetables to the pan.

5 Cover and cook in the oven for 2 hours 30 minutes until very tender, checking on the amount of liquid during cooking and adding more boiling water if required. Remove the bouquet garni and serve.

Per serving 1416kJ/336kcal (17%), 9.4g fat (13%), 2.7g saturates (14%), 7.9g sugars (9%), 1.22g salt (20%)

**Love your leftovers**
Freeze leftover wine in ice cube trays for use in cooking. Once frozen, transfer to a freezer bag. Add a cube or two to a casserole or stew for added flavour.

# Hungarian beef goulash

Paprika is the signature ingredient of this traditional beef stew from Hungary, and gives the dish its distinctive flavour

1 tbsp vegetable oil

¼ x 200g pack Be good to yourself smoked bacon medallions by Sainsbury's, diced

6 onions, about 750g total weight, chopped

2 tbsp paprika

750g braising steak from Sainsbury's meat counter, cut into 4cm cubes

2 garlic cloves, finely chopped

½ tsp caraway seeds

2 tomatoes, deseeded and chopped

2 green peppers, deseeded and sliced

freshly ground black pepper

1 egg

45g plain flour

1 Heat the oil in a flameproof casserole, add the bacon and stir for 3-5 minutes until it is lightly golden. Stir in the onions. Cut a piece of foil to fit the casserole, then cover the mixture and put on the lid. Cook over a low heat, stirring occasionally, for 20-25 minutes, until the onions are soft and translucent.

2 Preheat the oven to 180°C/160°C fan/gas 4. Stir the paprika into the onions and bacon and cook for 2 minutes; don't let the paprika scorch. Add the steak, garlic, caraway seeds and 500ml water and stir. Bring to the boil, stirring, then cover and cook in the oven for 1 hour-1 hour 30 minutes until the beef is almost tender.

3 Stir the tomatoes and peppers into the goulash. Cover and cook for 30-45 minutes more until the meat is very soft and the stew rich and thick. Season with black pepper.

4 To make the dumplings, lightly beat the egg in a small bowl. Put the flour in another bowl, then stir in the egg. Transfer the goulash to the top of the stove and heat to boiling. Using 2 teaspoons, drop spoonfuls of the dumpling mix into the goulash and simmer for 5-7 minutes until cooked.

5 Ladle the goulash and dumplings into warm soup bowls and serve.

**Per serving** 1516kJ/360kcal (18%), 8.6g fat (12%), 2.3g saturates (12%), 9.8g sugars (11%), 0.62g salt (10%)

SERVES 8
PREP 30 minutes
COOK 1 hour 30 minutes–
1 hour 50 minutes,
depending on the weight
of the joint

# Maple and mustard crusted rib of beef

Cooking the meat on the bone adds flavour and keeps the joint moist in this impressive dish, and the mustard crust complements it well

2-rib Scottish beef bone-in rib, about 2kg, from Sainsbury's meat counter

3 tbsp rapeseed oil, plus extra for greasing

freshly ground black pepper

75g fine breadcrumbs

1 tbsp finely chopped rosemary

2 tbsp finely chopped flat-leaf parsley

small bunch of fresh thyme leaves, finely chopped

3 large carrots, roughly chopped into small rounds

500g shallots

2 celery sticks, roughly chopped

4 garlic cloves

400ml red wine

2 tbsp maple syrup by Sainsbury's

3 tbsp Dijon mustard, plus 1 tsp extra

100ml port

500g pouch Signature beef stock by Sainsbury's, heated

4 tsp cornflour, mixed to a paste with a little warm water

2 tsp redcurrant jelly

1 Take the beef out of the fridge 2–3 hours before cooking to allow it to come to room temperature. Preheat the oven to 230°C/210°C fan/gas 8. Rub the beef with 2 tablespoons of oil and season with black pepper. Fry the beef in a large frying pan until just coloured all over. Remove from the heat. Place the breadcrumbs, rosemary, parsley and half the thyme in a large bowl. Season with black pepper, mix well and press the mixture over the fat side of the beef until evenly coated.

2 Place the carrots, shallots, celery, garlic and remaining thyme and oil in a large roasting tin and mix well. Place the beef on top of the vegetables and cover with an oiled sheet of foil. Roast in the oven for 20 minutes. Then remove the tin from the oven and add half the red wine and a splash of water. Replace the foil. Reduce the oven temperature to 200°C/180°C fan/gas 6 and roast for a further 40 minutes, adding more water if necessary.

3 Meanwhile, mix the maple syrup and mustard in a small bowl. Remove the tin from the oven and take off the foil. Coat the crust with the maple and mustard mixture, and press down lightly. Return the tin to the oven for the rest of the cooking time. Remove from the oven. Place the beef on a serving dish, loosely cover with foil and leave to rest for at least 20 minutes.

4 Remove and discard any excess fat from the tin. Add the port, stock and remaining red wine. Place the tin over a high heat and bring to the boil. Then strain, reserving the vegetables. Reduce the heat, add the cornflour mixture and cook the sauce until thickened. Then add the jelly and remaining mustard, season with black pepper and serve with the beef and reserved vegetables.

**Per serving** 2325kJ/556kcal (28%), 27.8g fat (40%), 10.9g saturates (55%), 11.3g sugars (13%), 1.07g salt (18%)

Beef

SERVES 8
PREP 30 minutes
COOK 2 hours 45 minutes–
3 hours 15 minutes,
plus resting

# Steak and kidney pie

A suet crust gives this pie a different finish

3 tbsp olive oil, plus extra
for greasing
2 onions, finely chopped
100g baby button mushrooms,
wiped, halved or quartered,
if necessary
600g braising steak by
Sainsbury's, cut into 2cm chunks
freshly ground black pepper

3 tbsp plain flour
600ml beef stock (made with
1/2 stock cube and boiling water)
large sprig of thyme
180g lamb kidneys (about 4),
from Sainsbury's meat counter
500g pack Chantenay carrots by
Sainsbury's, cooked according to
pack instructions, to serve

FOR THE SUET
CRUST PASTRY
200g self-raising flour
100g light vegetable suet
1/2 tsp salt
flour, for dusting
1 egg, beaten,
for glazing

1 In a pan, heat 1 tablespoon of oil and fry the onions for 5 minutes until softened but not browned. Add the mushrooms and fry for 3-4 minutes until they begin to colour in places. Remove the vegetables from the pan with a slotted spoon and set aside.

2 Toss the diced steak in 2 tablespoons of seasoned flour. Heat the remaining oil in the pan, on a high heat, and fry the meat, until browned. Take care not to overcrowd the pan or the meat will begin to steam rather than brown. Remove the meat as it cooks and add it to the vegetables. Once the meat is seared, return it and the vegetables to the pan. Cover with the beef stock. Season with black pepper, add the thyme and bring to the boil. When boiled, reduce the heat to low, cover and cook for 2 hours-2 hours 30 minutes until tender.

3 For the pastry, rub together the flour and suet until it resembles crumbs. Add the salt and enough cold water to bring the mixture together to a soft dough, following the instructions on the pack. Wrap in cling film. Rest the dough for at least 1 hour in the fridge.

4 Preheat the oven to 180°C/160°C fan/gas 4. Trim the kidneys of any skin, using a pair of scissors. Cut out the central core and remove and discard the sinews. Cut the kidneys into small pieces and add them to the stew. Roll out the pastry on a floured surface so that it is about 5cm larger all around than the top of a 2.5 litre pie dish. It should be 3-5mm thick. Cut out a strip of pastry about 2.5cm from the edge to make a collar.

5 Oil the dish and fill it with the pie filling. Dampen the edge of the dish with a little water, fit the pastry strips all the way around and press down firmly. Brush the pastry collar with a little of the beaten egg, then top with the pastry lid, using a pie funnel to help support it. Trim any excess pastry and press down around the edge to seal using the prongs of a fork. Brush the pie with beaten egg. Bake in the middle of the oven for 40-45 minutes until golden. Remove from the oven and allow to cool for at least 5 minutes before serving with the Chantenay carrots.

Per serving 1871kJ/446kcal (22%), 17.6g fat (25%), 6.5g saturates (33%), 6.9g sugars (8%), 0.84g salt (14%)

124

# Herby steak and vegetable pie

The filling for this pie makes a delicious stand-alone casserole

**FOR THE FILLING**

1 large potato, peeled and cut into bite-sized pieces

2 carrots, peeled and cut into bite-sized pieces

1 parsnip, peeled and cut into bite-sized pieces

500g braising steak, chopped into bite-sized pieces

1 tbsp olive oil

1 onion, peeled and finely chopped

1 tbsp plain flour

1 tbsp Worcestershire sauce

200ml beef stock (made with ½ stock cube and boiling water)

150ml red wine

2 tbsp finely chopped rosemary leaves

1 bay leaf

freshly ground black pepper

**FOR THE PASTRY**

250g ready rolled light puff pastry by Sainsbury's

flour, for dusting

1 egg, lightly beaten, for glazing

**1** Boil the potato, carrots and parsnip chunks in a saucepan of water for 15 minutes until soft. Drain and set aside. Put the meat in a large, non-stick frying pan with ½ tablespoon of the olive oil, and cook over a high heat for 5–8 minutes until it has coloured all over. Remove with a slotted spoon, cover and set aside.

**2** Heat the remaining oil in the frying pan over a low heat. Add the onion and fry gently for about 5 minutes until soft and translucent. Stir in the flour, and continue to cook for a further 2 minutes. Increase the heat a little, and add the Worcestershire sauce, stock, wine, rosemary and bay leaf. Bring to the boil, reduce the heat slightly and return the meat to the pan. Cover and simmer gently over a low heat for about 30 minutes, stirring occasionally. Stir through the cooked vegetables and season with black pepper.

**3** Meanwhile, preheat the oven to 200°C/180°C fan/gas 6. Remove the bay leaf from the meat and spoon the filling into the pie dish. Cut the pastry so that it is about 5cm larger all around than the top of a 1.2 litre pie dish. Cut out a strip of pastry about 2.5cm in from the edge to make a collar. Dampen the edge of the dish with a little water, fit the pastry strip all the way around and press down firmly.

**4** Brush the pastry collar with a little of the beaten egg, then top with the pastry lid. Trim away the excess pastry, then using your finger and thumb, pinch the edges of the pastry together to seal. Brush the top of the pie with beaten egg, then cut 2 slits to allow steam to escape. Bake for 30 minutes, or until puffed up and golden. Serve hot.

**Per serving** 1672kJ/398kcal (20%), 13.2g fat (19%), 5g saturates (25%), 6.5g sugars (7%), 0.95g salt (16%)

# The perfect steak

Frying steaks is a simple method that produces great results. Remove the steaks from the fridge 30 minutes before cooking. Total cooking time will vary from about 10–12 minutes for medium to 12–14 for well done

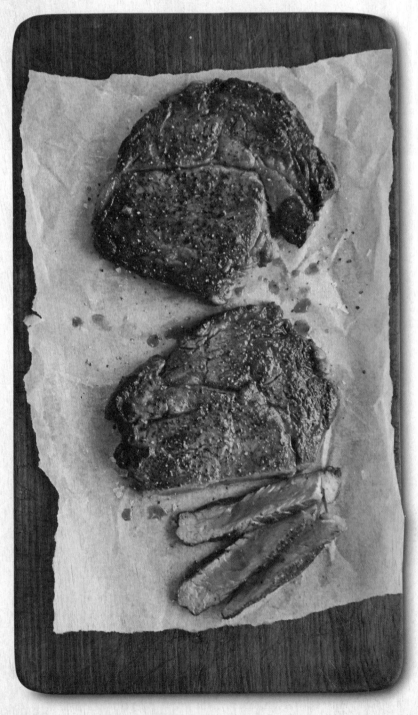

1 Preheat a heavy-based frying pan over a high heat. Add 1–2 tablespoons butter or oil to the pan, heating until it shimmers. Pat the steaks dry and carefully lay them in the pan, ensuring each steak is in contact with the pan by pressing it down all over with a slotted spatula.

2 Turn the heat down slightly to avoid the fat burning, then leave the steaks untouched for 1–2 minutes before lifting them with tongs to check the underside. Turn the steaks over onto the uncooked side.

3 Season the browned sides with black pepper. Leave the steaks to cook for a few minutes (how long depends on personal preference), then flip them over and season the other browned sides to taste. Continue frying the steaks, flipping them every 1–2 minutes, until cooked through and drops of juice are visible on the surface. Remove from the pan and rest for 3–4 minutes on a warm plate before serving.

# Sauces for steak

All these sauces make excellent accompaniments to steak. Ensure all fresh herbs are washed before use

## Blue cheese sauce

**MAKES** 250ml

Heat 25g unsalted butter in a small frying pan over a low heat. Add 2 finely diced shallots and cook for 5 minutes, or until softened. Add 4 tbsp dry white wine, 1 tbsp brandy and 2 tbsp beef stock. Bring to the boil and cook until the liquid has reduced by half. Mix in 200ml double cream and reduce the heat to a simmer. Cook for 5 minutes, then whisk in a further 25g unsalted butter and 100g crumbled Roquefort cheese. Remove from the heat and strain through a sieve.

## Chimichurri sauce

**MAKES** 250ml

Place 12 tbsp olive oil, 2 tbsp lemon juice, 3 tbsp red wine vinegar, 30g chopped flat-leaf parsley, 4 tbsp chopped coriander leaves, 2 tbsp chopped oregano leaves, 4 chopped garlic cloves and 2 tsp dried red chilli flakes in a large serving bowl and mix well to combine. Cover with cling film and chill for at least 1 hour to allow the flavours to develop.

## Mustard cream sauce

**MAKES** 250ml

Combine 150ml soured cream and 4 tbsp mayonnaise with 1¹/₂ tsp horseradish sauce and 1¹/₂ tsp sugar. Season with freshly ground black pepper.

## Hollandaise sauce

**MAKES** 200ml

Bring 1 tbsp white wine vinegar and 1 tbsp lemon juice to the boil in a small saucepan. Remove from the heat. Meanwhile, blend 3 large egg yolks with freshly ground black pepper in a food processor or blender for 1 minute. With the motor running, slowly add the lemon juice and vinegar mixture. Melt 175g unsalted butter until it begins to foam. Remove from the heat. With the food processor running, gradually add the butter to form a thick sauce. Serve immediately.

## Red wine sauce

**MAKES** 250ml

Boil 200ml dry red wine in the pan used to cook the steak. Simmer until the juices are reduced by half. Stir in 150g crème fraîche. Add 2 tbsp chopped parsley and season to taste.

## Herb butter

**MAKES** 150ml

In a bowl, combine 125g softened unsalted butter with 1 tsp Dijon mustard, 1 tbsp lemon juice, 1 finely chopped garlic clove, 1 finely chopped shallot, 1 tbsp snipped chives, 1 tbsp chopped parsley, 1 tbsp chopped basil and 1 tbsp chopped mint until well mixed. Transfer the mixture to a sheet of greaseproof & non-stick baking paper by Sainsbury's and mould it into a roll. Wrap the roll with the paper and twist the ends to seal. Chill in the fridge until the butter is firm.

## Béarnaise sauce

**MAKES** 200ml

Boil 2 tbsp white wine vinegar and 2 tbsp white wine with 2 small, finely chopped shallots, 1 tbsp chopped tarragon and 1 tsp crushed black peppercorns in a heavy non-stick saucepan for 2 minutes, or until reduced by at least half. Strain through a sieve and set aside, covered, to cool. Put 3 egg yolks and 1 tbsp water in a heatproof bowl, and set over a pan of barely simmering water, without allowing the bowl to touch the water. Whisk in the cooled wine liquid, then gradually whisk in 200g softened, cubed unsalted butter until it has melted into the sauce. Season with freshly ground black pepper and up to 1 tbsp lemon juice. Stir in a further 2 tbsp chopped tarragon and serve immediately.

# Cinnamon and ginger beef with noodles

A quick dish full of Oriental spices, with the flavour of cinnamon permeating throughout

450g extra lean beef stir fry by Sainsbury's

2 tsp ground cinnamon

1 tbsp sunflower oil

1 onion, sliced

5cm piece of fresh root ginger, peeled and shredded

1 red chilli, deseeded and finely chopped

2 garlic cloves, finely chopped

1 tbsp fish sauce

1 tbsp toasted sesame oil by Sainsbury's

200g pack Taste the Difference speciality mushrooms by Sainsbury's, trimmed or chopped

200g pack trimmed mange tout

2 x 300g pack Quick to cook udon noodles by Sainsbury's

**1** Place the steak in a bowl, sprinkle over the cinnamon, coat and set aside. Heat the sunflower oil in a wok, add the onion and stir-fry over a high heat for 1 minute. Add the ginger and chilli and stir-fry for a further minute.

**2** Add the beef, garlic, fish sauce and sesame oil and continue to cook, stirring, until the meat is cooked through with no pink colour remaining. Add the mushrooms and mange tout and continue to stir-fry for a further 1–2 minutes.

**3** Add the noodles and stir-fry for about 3 minutes until the noodles become sticky. Serve hot immediately.

**Per serving** 2370kJ/562kcal (28%), 11.3g fat (16%), 2.4g saturates (12%), 7.2g sugars (8%), 1.55g salt (26%)

### Cook's tip
Always cook quickly over a high heat when using a wok, and have all your ingredients to hand.

# Spaghetti and meatballs

Spaghetti paired with homemade meatballs, fresh herbs and a tomato sauce are a firm family favourite

**FOR THE MEATBALLS**
500g pack beef mince 5% fat
by Sainsbury's
1 small onion, finely chopped
1 garlic clove, crushed
50g fresh white breadcrumbs
15g Parmesan cheese, grated
1 tbsp finely chopped thyme
1 tbsp finely chopped oregano
2 tbsp finely chopped
flat-leaf parsley
1 egg, beaten
freshly ground black pepper
2 tbsp olive oil

**FOR THE SAUCE**
1 onion, finely chopped
2 garlic cloves, crushed
2 x 390g cartons chopped
tomatoes by Sainsbury's
250ml chicken or beef stock
(made with 1/2 stock cube
and boiling water)
2 tbsp finely chopped
flat-leaf parsley
freshly ground black pepper
300g spaghetti
10g Parmesan cheese shavings,
to serve

1 For the meatballs, place all the ingredients, except the oil, in a large bowl, season well with black pepper and mix thoroughly with your fingertips. Form 16 equally sized meatballs, cover with cling film and allow to rest for 30 minutes. This will help them retain their shape while cooking. Heat the oil in a large frying pan with high sides. Fry the meatballs over a medium-high heat for 4–6 minutes, turning during cooking, until they are browned, but not cooked through. Remove them from the heat and set aside.

2 To prepare the sauce, add the onion to the same pan and cook over a low heat for 5 minutes until softened but not brown. Scrape up any residue left in the pan from the meatballs, as this will flavour the sauce. Add the garlic and cook for 1–2 minutes. Add the tomatoes, stock and chopped parsley and season with black pepper. Bring the sauce to the boil, reduce the heat to a low simmer and cook for 30 minutes until reduced and thickened. If the sauce looks too thick, add a little water. You can also make the sauce smoother, if you prefer, by either mashing it with a potato masher or using a hand-held blender.

3 Cook the spaghetti according to the pack instructions. Add the meatballs to the sauce 12 minutes before the end of the cooking time. Turn them so that they are well covered in the sauce, reduce the heat to a low simmer and cook, covered, until the meatballs are cooked through, with no pink remaining. Drain the spaghetti, once cooked, and toss with the meatballs and sauce. Serve with the Parmesan shavings scattered over.

**Per serving** 2849kJ/675kcal (34%), 15.4g fat (22%), 5.0g saturates (25%), 12.2g sugars (14%), 1.38g salt (23%)

**SERVES** 6
**PREP** 30 minutes
**COOK** 30 minutes,
plus resting

# Cottage pie

Traditionally a recipe to use up the leftover meat and potatoes from a Sunday roast, this modern version uses beef mince, with the added twist of leeks in the mashed potato topping

750g pack beef mince 10% fat by Sainsbury's
1 tbsp sunflower oil
1 large onion, chopped
1 garlic clove, crushed
2 carrots, sliced
90ml dry red wine
2 tbsp plain flour
250ml beef stock (made with ½ stock cube and boiling water)

1 tbsp Worcestershire sauce by Sainsbury's
2 tbsp chopped flat-leaf parsley
1 tbsp dried thyme
freshly ground black pepper

**FOR THE POTATO AND LEEK MASH**
1.25kg Maris Piper potatoes, peeled and cut into chunks

2 large leeks, cut in half lengthways, sliced
30ml semi-skimmed milk
20g sunflower spread
freshly ground black pepper

1 Preheat the oven to 200°C/180°C fan/gas 6. To make the leek mash, place the potatoes in a large pan, cover with cold water and bring to the boil. Cook for 12 minutes, add the leeks and cook for a further 5 minutes, or until the potatoes are tender. Drain and mash together with milk and sunflower spread, and season with black pepper.

2 To make the filling, fry the beef mince in a large frying pan over a medium-high heat for 5 minutes, or until lightly coloured. Pour off the fat, remove the meat from the pan and set aside.

3 In the same pan, heat the oil. Fry the onion and garlic, stirring for 3-5 minutes, or until softened, then add the carrots. Add the cooked mince to the pan and stir together.

4 Add the wine, increase the heat to high and cook for 2-3 minutes. Stir in the flour once the wine has evaporated. Stir in the stock, Worcestershire sauce, parsley and thyme, and season with black pepper. Bring to the boil, then reduce the heat to low and simmer for 5 minutes.

5 Spoon the filling into a large ovenproof dish and top with the mashed potatoes. Place the dish on an oven tray and bake for 30 minutes, or until the mashed potatoes are golden. Leave to rest for 5 minutes, then serve straight from the dish.

**Per serving** 2217kJ/527kcal (26%), 17.1g fat (24%), 6.4g saturates (32%), 8.1g sugars (9%), 0.91g salt (15%)

**Get ahead**
The pie can be made up to 24 hours in advance and stored, covered, in the fridge. Ensure the dish is piping hot before serving.

# Gnocchi with Bolognese sauce

Bolognese sauce is a favourite partner for pasta and this sauce can be used as a base for a variety of dishes

1 tbsp olive oil

1 onion, finely chopped

2 garlic cloves, finely chopped

500g minced beef 5% fat
by Sainsbury's

1 tsp dried oregano

1 tsp dried marjoram

390g carton chopped tomatoes

1 tbsp tomato purée mixed
with 110ml boiling water

150ml red wine

1 bay leaf

freshly ground black pepper

500g fresh gnocchi
by Sainsbury's

50g fresh white breadcrumbs
from day-old farmhouse bread
by Sainsbury's

40g finely grated
Parmesan cheese

2 x 170g bags watercress,
spinach and rocket salad
by Sainsbury's, to serve

**1** Heat the oil in a large pan over a medium heat and fry the onion for 5 minutes. Add the garlic and cook for 2 minutes.

**2** Stir the meat into the pan and cook for 5 minutes, breaking it up with a wooden spoon, until it has been allowed to colour. Stir in the dried herbs, tomatoes, tomato purée liquid, wine and bay leaf. Season with black pepper and bring to the boil, then reduce the heat, partially cover and simmer gently for 1 hour, stirring occasionally. Preheat the oven to 190°C/170°C fan/gas 5.

**3** Put the gnocchi in a shallow ovenproof dish. Mix the breadcrumbs, Parmesan cheese and plenty of black pepper in a bowl.

**4** Pour the Bolognese sauce over the gnocchi and sprinkle with the cheesy breadcrumbs. Place the dish on a baking tray and bake for 15 minutes, or until the crumbs are crispy. Spoon onto plates and serve with the salad.

**Per serving** 2472kJ/586kcal (29%), 12.6g fat (18%), 5.2g saturates (26%), 8g sugars (9%), 2.19g salt (37%)

**Get ahead**
Assemble this recipe a day in advance, cover and refrigerate. Simply bake as in step 4 to finish.

SERVES 4
PREP 40-50 minutes
COOK 3 hours 30 minutes–
4 hours

# Indonesian beef curry

Well worth the long cooking time, this Indonesian speciality – known as beef 'rendang' – was originally made with water buffalo

**FOR THE CURRY PASTE**
1.25cm piece cinnamon stick
6 cloves
1 lemongrass stalk, trimmed
and roughly chopped
3 shallots, quartered
5cm piece fresh root ginger,
peeled and roughly chopped
3 garlic cloves, peeled
3 red chillies, finely chopped
½ tsp ground turmeric

**FOR THE BEEF**
400ml tin coconut milk light
by Sainsbury's
2 bay leaves
500g braising steak from
Sainsbury's meat counter,
in 5cm cubes

**TO SERVE**
360g basmati rice, cooked
according to pack instructions
1 tbsp fresh coriander
leaves, washed

1 First, prepare the curry paste. Crumble or break the cinnamon stick into small pieces and put them in a mortar with the cloves. Pound them with the pestle until coarsely crushed. Put the cinnamon and cloves in a food processor with the remaining curry paste ingredients. Process to a coarse paste. If the mixture is very thick, add about 2 tablespoons of the coconut milk.

2 Combine the curry paste and coconut milk in a wok or heavy-based frying pan and stir until well mixed. Add the bay leaves and bring to the boil over a high heat, stirring occasionally.

3 Reduce the heat to medium and cook the sauce, stirring occasionally, for about 15 minutes. Add the beef, stir and return to the boil over a high heat. Reduce the heat to medium and simmer, uncovered, stirring occasionally, for 2 hours.

4 Reduce the heat to very low and continue cooking for 1 hour 30 minutes–2 hours until the beef is tender and the sauce quite thick. Stir frequently to prevent sticking.

5 Skim off all the fat. The sauce will be very thick. Arrange a bed of cooked rice on warm plates or shallow bowls, spoon the curried beef on top, and garnish with the coriander.

**Per serving** 2601kJ/616kcal (31%), 12.3g fat (18%), 7.3g saturates (37%), 4.2g sugars (5%), 1.57g salt (26%)

# Lamb with artichokes and broad beans

A stew full of flavour and green vegetables, this dish is great for serving a crowd

650g lamb steak (about 6 steaks) from Sainsbury's meat counter, cut into chunks
freshly ground black pepper
1½ tbsp olive oil
2 onions, roughly chopped
3 carrots, peeled and roughly chopped
1 tbsp plain flour

120ml dry white wine
900ml vegetable stock (made with 1 stock cube and boiling water)
a few sprigs of rosemary, washed
1 lemon, zest and juice
2 x 400g tins cooked artichoke hearts in water by Sainsbury's, drained and quartered

350g frozen broad beans
bunch of dill, washed and finely chopped
400g baguette, torn into chunks, to serve

**1** Preheat the oven to 180°C/160°C fan/gas 4. Season the meat with black pepper. Heat 1 tablespoon of oil in a large flameproof casserole over a high heat, add the lamb (in batches, if necessary), and cook for 6–8 minutes until no longer pink. Remove from the casserole and set aside.

**2** Heat the remaining oil in the casserole over a medium heat, add the onions and cook for 3–4 minutes until soft. Season with black pepper, add the carrots and cook for a further 5 minutes. Sprinkle over the flour, stir and cook for a couple of minutes. Add the wine, increase the heat and cook the sauce for a minute.

**3** Add the lamb, stock, rosemary, lemon juice and zest. Bring to the boil, cover and put in the oven for 1 hour. Check occasionally that it's not drying out and top up with a little hot water if needed. Stir through the artichokes and broad beans and cook for a further 30 minutes, or until the vegetables are tender. Taste, season with black pepper and add the dill to taste. Serve with crusty bread.

**Per serving** 2281kJ/544kcal (27%), 23.2g fat (33%), 10.5g saturates (53%), 9.5g sugars (11%), 1.38g salt (23%)

# Moussaka

A good moussaka may take a while to prepare, but the time taken to get the sauces right is well worth it

3 tbsp olive oil
1 onion, chopped
2 garlic cloves, chopped
1 tsp ground cinnamon
500g pack lamb mince 20% fat by Sainsbury's
1 tbsp tomato purée
100ml red wine

390g carton chopped tomatoes by Sainsbury's
2 tbsp flat-leaf parsley, washed and chopped
2 aubergines, cut into 5mm slices
2 Maris Piper potatoes, skins on
75g unsalted butter

75g plain flour
570ml semi-skimmed milk
2 medium eggs
50g Parmesan cheese, grated
3 x 135g bags crispy leaf salad by Sainsbury's, to serve

**1** Preheat the oven to 180°C/160°C fan/gas 4. Heat 1 tablespoon of oil in a pan and gently fry the onion over a medium heat until translucent. Add the garlic and cinnamon and fry for 1 minute. Add the lamb and fry for about 5 minutes until coloured. Drain and discard the oil.

**2** Stir the tomato purée through the mince and add the wine, tomatoes and parsley. Reduce the heat and simmer for 30 minutes, then season with black pepper.

**3** Meanwhile, brush 2 oven trays with 1 tablespoon oil. Arrange the aubergine slices on them in a single layer. Brush with the remaining oil and bake in the oven for 25 minutes, turning once during cooking.

**4** In the meantime, place the potatoes in a pan, cover with water and bring to the boil. Simmer for 10 minutes until still slightly firm in the centre. Drain and cool, then peel and slice.

**5** Melt the butter in a small pan over a low heat. Stir in the flour and cook for 1 minute. Gradually add the milk, stirring until you have a smooth sauce. Season with black pepper, then bring to the boil, before reducing the heat and simmering for 2-3 minutes, stirring frequently. Remove from the heat and beat in the eggs.

**6** Place the potato slices in a single layer in the bottom of a 3.2 litre ovenproof dish. Layer on half the aubergine slices. Top with the mince mixture then add the remaining aubergine slices. Pour the white sauce evenly over the top and sprinkle with the cheese. Cover with foil and bake for 20 minutes. Remove the foil and bake for a further 25 minutes until the top is golden. Serve hot with a green salad.

**Per serving** 1936kJ/465kcal (23%), 29.2g fat (42%), 13.8g saturates (69%), 10.1g sugars (11%), 0.57g salt (10%)

**Get ahead**
Make the meat sauce the day before. Cover it and keep it chilled until you need it.

# Lamb tagine with cauliflower 'couscous'

Using vegetables as a substitute for pulses and grains is becoming increasingly popular – try this delicious cauliflower alternative to couscous

650g lamb steak from Sainsbury's meat counter, cut into chunks
2 garlic cloves, finely chopped
5cm piece fresh root ginger, peeled and grated
freshly ground black pepper
½ tsp ground cinnamon
½ tsp turmeric
1 onion, grated
1 tbsp olive oil

450g carrots, peeled or scrubbed and roughly chopped
900ml lamb stock (made with 1 stock cube and boiling water)
120g from 180g jar preserved lemon slices by Sainsbury's, flesh discarded and skin finely sliced, or 1 fresh lemon, zest and juice
handful of fresh flat-leaf parsley, washed and finely chopped

**FOR THE 'COUSCOUS'**
1 cauliflower, broken into large florets
1 tbsp olive oil
1–2 tsp ground cumin
freshly ground black pepper

1  Toss the lamb with the garlic, ginger, pepper, cinnamon, turmeric and onion. Heat the oil in a large, heavy-based pan, add the lamb mixture and cook over a medium heat for 10 minutes until the lamb is sealed. Add the carrots and stir to combine. Pour over the stock, bring to the boil, cover and simmer over a low heat for 1 hour–1 hour 30 minutes until the lamb is tender, topping up with hot water as needed; alternatively transfer to a casserole dish and bake in an oven preheated to 180°C/160°C fan/gas 4 for 1 hour 30 minutes.

2 Preheat the oven to 200°C/180°C fan/gas 6. Toss the cauliflower with the oil and cumin and season with black pepper. Transfer to a roasting tin and bake for 10 minutes, or until just turning golden. Remove the cauliflower from the oven and leave to cool completely. Transfer to a food processor, or use a hand blender, and pulse until it resembles grains; don't overwork or it will become mushy.

3 Stir the preserved lemons or zest and juice into the lamb for the last 15 minutes of cooking, then stir through the parsley when ready to serve.

**Per serving** 1483kJ/354kcal (18%), 14.3g fat (20%), 4.2g saturates (21%), 9.7g sugars (11%), 1.21g salt (20%)

SERVES 4
PREP 30 minutes,
plus marinating
COOK 4 hours

# Spiced lamb and houmous wraps

A superb mix of textures and punchy flavours make up this Lebanese-inspired meal

400g pack boneless lamb shoulder by Sainsbury's

**FOR THE SPICE RUB**
½ tsp ground cinnamon
½ tsp ground coriander
¼ tsp ground cumin
1 tsp dried mint
freshly ground black pepper
2 tbsp olive oil

**TO SERVE**
8 plain tortilla wraps by Sainsbury's
260g bag young spinach
1 quantity houmous (see p22)
1 lemon, cut into wedges

1 For the spice rub, mix together the spices, herbs and pepper and stir into 1 tablespoon of oil. Rub into the lamb and leave for at least 30 minutes, or covered in the fridge overnight. Preheat the oven to 160°C/140°C fan/gas 3. In a large, heavy-based frying pan, heat the remaining olive oil, add the lamb and cook over a medium-high heat for 5-10 minutes, or until browned all over.

2 Place the lamb in a large roasting tin, cover it with foil and cook for 4 hours, removing the foil for the last 15 minutes of cooking. Remove from the oven, cover and leave to rest for at least 20 minutes.

3 Heat the wraps in the oven according to the pack instructions. Shred the lamb and transfer to a serving plate. Remove the wraps from the oven, top with the fresh spinach, houmous and lamb, and add a squeeze of lemon. Roll or fold to serve.

**Per serving** 2871kJ/686kcal (34%), 33.4g fat (48%), 11.9g saturates (60%), 2g sugars (2%), 1.3g salt (22%)

# Potatoes

< **King Edward** is a famous British variety with a full flavour and floury texture. It is an excellent all-rounder in the kitchen, and is particularly good for roasting and mashing.

^ **Desiree** is an all-purpose variety with pink skin and yellow, creamy flesh. It makes great mash, and can also be baked, roasted, boiled or fried.

^ **Sweet** potatoes have moist, sweet flesh that lends itself to baking, boiling, mashing and roasting. They can also be used in cakes and pies.

> **Charlotte** is a high-quality, waxy variety with a smooth, slightly sticky flesh and a fresh, mild flavour. It is best boiled or steamed in its skin.

^ **Maris Piper**, a popular floury potato, has a full flavour and fluffy texture. It is excellent for mashing, baking, roasting and for making chips.

^ **Jersey Royal** is a famous heritage variety with a smooth, waxy flesh and distinctive rich, buttery flavour.

^ **Baby** potatoes are firm-textured, and taste delicious boiled or steamed, in salads or served as new potatoes. Leave the skins on to add texture.

^ **Vivaldi** is a multi-purpose variety with smooth flesh and a distinct buttery flavour. It makes great mashed potato.

^ **Anya** is a hybrid variety with a waxy texture and slightly nutty flavour. Best boiled or steamed in its skin, it can also be fried.

## Waxy or floury?

It's important to choose the right potato for the job, as they vary so much in texture. All-purpose potatoes, such as Desiree, can be cooked all ways, while others suit particular methods. Waxy types, such as Charlotte, Anya and Jersey Royal, are ideal for boiling and steaming. Floury types, such as King Edward and Maris Piper, are the best for baking or mashing.

# Pearl barley, spinach and lamb pot

One-pot cooking at its best, this dish is easy to make and full of flavour

80g pearl barley
1 tbsp olive oil
1 onion, finely chopped
2 garlic cloves, finely chopped
3 carrots, peeled and diced
3 celery stalks, washed
and diced
a few stalks of thyme
450g lamb steak (about
8 small steaks or 4 larger
steaks) from Sainsbury's
meat counter

1.2 litres lamb stock
(made with 1 stock cube
and boiling water)
2 x 260g bags young spinach
by Sainsbury's, roughly chopped
freshly ground black pepper

1 Place the barley in a pan and cover with cold water. Bring to the boil, drain and rinse with cold water. Cover and set aside.

2 Heat the oil in a large heavy-based pan, add the onion and cook over a low heat until it softens. Add the garlic, carrot, celery and thyme and cook for a further 10 minutes. Add the lamb to the pan and cover with the stock. Bring to the boil and skim off any foam that comes to the surface. Reduce to a simmer, add the pearl barley and cook gently for 1 hour until the lamb is tender and cooked through and the pearl barley is tender. Top up with more stock or water if needed.

3 Remove the lamb from the pan, cover and leave to cool slightly. Meanwhile, add the spinach to the pan and cook for 5 minutes, or until it has wilted. Return the lamb to the pot and stir carefully to combine, then taste and season with black pepper. Ladle into bowls and serve.

**Per serving** 1691kJ/404kcal (20%), 20.5g fat (29%), 7.4g saturates (37%), 9g sugars (10%), 1.43g salt (24%)

## Cook's tip
This will taste even better the next day; cover and put in the fridge once cooled and reheat thoroughly when required.

**SERVES** 6
**PREP** 45-50 minutes
**COOK** 2 hours-2 hours
15 minutes

# Navarin of lamb

The origin of the name of the dish may have come from the inclusion of turnips, or 'navet' in French

400g pack shallots by Sainsbury's
2 tbsp vegetable oil
650g lean lamb steaks by Sainsbury's, cut into 2cm cubes
freshly ground black pepper
2 tbsp plain flour

1 tbsp tomato purée
2 garlic cloves, finely chopped
5g bouquet garni by Sainsbury's
500ml lamb stock (made with 1 stock cube and boiling water)
375g classic round tomatoes
250g baby turnips, or turnips, cut into chunks

2 x 270g packs mixed fine green beans and Chantenay carrots, washed
750g baby potatoes
150g frozen peas
leaves from 4-5 parsley sprigs, washed and finely chopped

1 Put the baby shallots in a bowl, cover with boiling water and let stand for 2 minutes. Drain, then peel. Heat the oil in a casserole. Add the whole shallots and stir for 5-7 minutes until golden. Remove and set aside.

2 Season the lamb with black pepper and add to the casserole, in batches if necessary. Cook over a high heat, stirring occasionally, for 3-5 minutes until evenly coloured. With a slotted spoon, transfer to a bowl. If you've cooked in batches, return all the cooked lamb to the pan, sprinkle with the flour, then stir to mix. Cook over a medium heat, stirring occasionally, for 2-3 minutes until the flour is coloured. Let the casserole cool slightly, then stir in the tomato purée, garlic and bouquet garni. Pour in enough stock to just cover, stir and bring to the boil. Cover with a lid and simmer for 1 hour.

3 Core the tomatoes and score an 'X' on the base of each. Immerse in boiling water until the skins start to split (8-15 seconds). Plunge at once into cold water. When cool, peel off the skins, cut in half, squeeze out and discard the seeds, then coarsely chop the flesh. Peel the turnips. Cut them into quarters or wedges, depending on their size, and trim off sharp edges with a small knife. Cut the beans into 2.5cm pieces. Peel the potatoes, or leave the skins on if you prefer, but wash thoroughly. If peeled, put them into a bowl of cold water.

4 With a slotted spoon, transfer the meat to a large bowl, then skim the fat from the sauce with a broad, shallow spoon. Strain the sauce back over the meat, then return both the meat and sauce to the casserole.

5 Drain the potatoes and add them to the casserole with the turnips, shallots, tomatoes and carrots. Pour in more stock to almost cover the meat and vegetables. Cover and simmer for 20-25 minutes until the potatoes are tender.

6 Add the peas and beans to the stew and simmer until they are just tender. Be sure not to cook the navarin for any longer than necessary to cook the vegetables through; they should retain their fresh crunch and bright colours. Season with black pepper. The sauce should be glossy and lightly thickened. Ladle the meat and vegetables on to warmed plates, moisten with the sauce, and sprinkle with parsley.

**Per serving** 1700kJ/404kcal (20%), 10.5g fat (15%), 2.5g saturates (13%), 12.8g sugars (14%), 0.92g salt (15%)

# Pork chops with sweet potato and green beans

The dense orange flesh of sweet potato marries well with tender pork

1 tbsp olive oil
1 tsp Cajun spice seasoning
freshly ground black pepper
2 x 450g packs British
pork chops by Sainsbury's,
some fat trimmed
1 large sweet potato, halved,
peeled and roughly chopped

150g cherry tomatoes
125g dwarf green
beans, trimmed
handful of fresh thyme leaves,
washed, to garnish

1  Preheat the oven to 200°C/180°C fan/gas 6. In a small bowl, combine half the oil with the Cajun seasoning. Season with black pepper and mix well.

2  Brush the chops with half the spice mix and place in a roasting tin. Add the sweet potato to the remaining spice mix and toss lightly to coat. Add the sweet potato to the tin. Cook in the oven for 30-40 minutes, or until the pork is cooked through with no pink remaining and the sweet potato is softened and golden.

3  Meanwhile, place the tomatoes and beans in a bowl and toss with the remaining oil. Add to the roasting tin for the last 10 minutes of cooking so they are just lightly coloured in places. Remove from the heat, sprinkle with thyme and serve hot.

**Per serving** 2659kJ/636kcal (32%), 34.9g fat (50%), 11.9g saturates (60%), 6.1g sugars (7%), 1.29g salt (22%)

# Szechuan sweet and sour spare ribs

The chilli-flavoured oil in this recipe adds depth to the classic sweet and sour flavour

4 tbsp soy sauce reduced salt by Sainsbury's

4 tbsp cider vinegar

3 tbsp honey

1 tbsp toasted sesame oil by Sainsbury's

1 tsp chilli paste by Sainsbury's

4 tbsp dry sherry

2 tbsp vegetable oil

1 dried red chilli

3 x 500g packs British pork ribs by Sainsbury's

1  To make the sweet and sour sauce, whisk the soy sauce, cider vinegar, honey, sesame oil, chilli paste and sherry in a small bowl. Cover with cling film and set aside.

2 Heat the vegetable oil in a heavy-based frying pan or wok, add the chilli and cook for 1 minute until darkened. Add 3-4 ribs and stir over a high heat for 2-3 minutes until coloured on all sides. Transfer to a plate. Working in batches, fry the remaining ribs in the same way.

3 Pour the oil out from the pan, leaving only about 1 tablespoon in the pan. Return the ribs to the pan, pour in enough water to completely cover and bring to the boil. Reduce the heat and cover the pan. Simmer for about 1 hour, stirring occasionally. The ribs are cooked through when there is no pink colour remaining, the meat has shrunk slightly on the bone and feels tender to the tip of a knife.

4 Discard the chilli and add the sauce to the pan. Simmer, stirring occasionally, for 25-30 minutes until the liquid is reduced to a thick, dark sauce and the ribs are glazed. If necessary, remove the ribs from the pan and reduce the sauce further by bringing to a quick boil.

5 Place the ribs on a warm serving plate and serve with the reduced sweet and sour sauce for dipping.

**Per serving** 1731kJ/415kcal (21%), 26.8g fat (38%), 9.1g saturates (46%), 19.1g sugars (21%), 0.94g salt (16%)

SERVES 4
PREP 10 minutes,
plus chilling
COOK 40-45 minutes

# Swedish meatballs with mashed potatoes and gravy

Traditionally served with mashed potatoes and lingonberry jam, but equally tasty with redcurrant jelly, these mild meatballs are a taste of Scandinavia

**FOR THE MEATBALLS**
500g pack British pork mince 5% fat by Sainsbury's
75g fresh white breadcrumbs
½ onion, finely grated
1 tbsp semi-skimmed milk
1 egg, beaten
1 tsp caster sugar
freshly ground black pepper
½ tsp ground allspice

1 tbsp chopped flat-leaf parsley, washed

**FOR THE MASHED POTATOES**
1kg Maris Piper or King Edward potatoes, peeled and cut into chunks
30ml semi-skimmed milk
25g unsalted butter
freshly ground black pepper

**FOR THE GRAVY**
1 heaped tbsp plain flour
250ml beef stock (made with ½ stock cube and boiling water)
1 tsp redcurrant jelly
1 tbsp single cream

1 In a large bowl, mix the pork, breadcrumbs, onion, milk, egg, sugar and seasoning until well combined. Cover and chill for at least 1 hour. Preheat the oven to 190°C/170°C fan/gas 5.

2 With damp hands, shape the pork mixture into walnut-sized balls. Place well apart on a baking tray. Bake in the oven, turning occasionally, for 35 minutes, or until the meatballs are golden all over, springy to the touch and cooked through with no pink remaining.

3 Place the potatoes in a large pan, cover with cold water and bring to the boil. Cook for 10-15 minutes until tender. Drain and mash together with the milk and butter, and season with black pepper.

4 Meanwhile, make the gravy. Sprinkle the flour into the baking tray used to cook the meatballs. Whisk it into the fat in the pan, then gradually whisk in the stock.

5 Place the baking tray over a gentle heat and cook the gravy until it thickens. Reduce to a simmer, add the redcurrant jelly and cream, and cook for a further 2-3 minutes. Check for seasoning and serve spooned over the meatballs and mashed potato.

**Per serving** 2355kJ/560kcal (28%), 16.4g fat (23%), 6.9g saturates (35%), 4.7g sugars (5%), 1.24g salt (21%)

# Ham, cheese and broccoli pancakes

This recipe uses ready-made pancakes to make a simple, cannelloni-style bake that's easier to assemble than the traditional pasta tubes

unsalted butter, for greasing
125g small broccoli florets
200g garlic and herb light soft
cheese by Sainsbury's
75ml single cream
120g pack Taste the Difference
Wiltshire cured ham,
finely chopped
20g finely grated Parmesan
cheese

8 ready-made plain pancakes
by Sainsbury's
freshly ground black pepper
50g Be good to yourself grated
mozzarella cheese 10% fat
by Sainsbury's
50g fresh breadcrumbs
170g bag Italian-style salad
by Sainsbury's, to serve

1  Preheat the oven to 180°C/160°C fan/gas 4. Grease an oven tray. Cook the broccoli in boiling water for 5 minutes. Drain.

2  Place the soft cheese and cream in a pan over a medium heat. Warm through, stirring, until the cheese has melted and the mixture is smooth. Stir in the broccoli, ham and Parmesan.

3  Place a pancake on a work surface and spread one-eighth of the filling over, seasoning with black pepper. Roll up and place on the oven tray. Repeat with the remaining pancakes and filling.

4  Sprinkle with mozzarella and breadcrumbs. Bake in the oven for 20 minutes. Serve the pancake cannelloni hot with a green salad.

**Per serving** 1988kJ/472kcal (24%), 14.8g fat (21%), 9.9g saturates (50%), 7.9g sugars (9%), 2.63g salt (44%)

**Why not try?**
As alternatives, why not try canned, drained tuna or cooked and finely chopped chicken instead of the ham in this recipe.

SERVES 8
PREP 10 minutes,
plus chilling
COOK 3 hours, plus resting

# Slow-cooked pork shoulder with cider gravy

This dish is cooked slowly to bring out the flavours of the pork, and enhanced by the fruity notes of the cider gravy

large crackling pork shoulder joint (about 2.2kg) by Sainsbury's, skin scored
1 tsp sea salt, for rubbing on joint

1 tbsp plain flour
400ml Original Somerset cider by Sainsbury's
pinch of caster sugar

**1** With a sharp knife, make criss-cross slits all over the skin of the pork, being careful not to cut through to the meat underneath. Rub the skin dry with kitchen paper and rub the salt into the scored skin.

**2** Preheat the oven to 190°C/170°C fan/gas 5. Check the weight of the joint and calculate the cooking time, allowing 30 minutes per 500g plus an extra 30 minutes. Place the joint on a rack over a roasting tin, put in the oven and roast for 30 minutes. Reduce the temperature to 170°C/150°C fan/gas 3 and continue cooking for the remainder of the calculated time.

**3** To tell when the joint is cooked, use a metal skewer and insert it into the centre of the joint; the juices that emerge when the skewer is removed should run clear. If there are traces of pink, roast it for another 10–15 minutes. Remove from the oven and let it rest for 15 minutes, covered in foil to keep warm.

**4** While the pork is resting, make the cider gravy. Spoon any excess fat out of the roasting tin and place the tin on the hob. Sprinkle over the flour and cook, stirring, for 1 minute. Add the cider and sugar and bring to the boil, stirring and scraping all the meat residue from the bottom of the tin. Let the liquid bubble for a minute then strain and serve with the pork. Remove the crackling to make carving easier.

**Per serving** 2534kJ/604kcal (30%), 28.1g fat (40%), 9.9g saturates (50%), 1.9g sugars (2%), 1.74g salt (29%)

# Spicy pork and beans

This is a sort of cowboy-style barbecue pork and beans, rich with dark, smoky flavours

1 tbsp olive oil
2 onions, finely chopped
2 garlic cloves, crushed
2 tsp plain flour
freshly ground black pepper
2 tsp smoked paprika
445g pack Basics diced pork shoulder by Sainsbury's
½ tsp dried oregano
1 tsp dark brown sugar

500ml pork stock (made with ½ stock cube and boiling water)
2 tbsp barbecue sauce by Sainsbury's
150g from a 395g tin mixed beans in mild chilli sauce by Sainsbury's
4 baking potatoes, cooked according to pack instructions, to serve

1 Preheat the oven to 200°C/180°C fan/gas 6. Heat ½ tablespoon of the oil in a large, heavy-based saucepan. Fry the onions over a medium heat for 5 minutes. Add the garlic and cook for a further minute. Cover and set aside.

2 Put the flour in a freezer bag with black pepper and 1 teaspoon of the smoked paprika. Toss the pork in it. Tip out into a sieve, shaking to remove excess flour.

3 Fry the pork in the remaining oil, in batches, for a couple of minutes on each side.

4 Return the onion mixture and stir in the remaining 1 teaspoon smoked paprika, the oregano and sugar. Mix in the stock and barbecue sauce and bring to the boil. Reduce to a gentle simmer and cook, covered, for 1 hour until the pork is cooked through with no pink remaining, adding the beans for the last 10 minutes of cooking time.

5 Meanwhile, prick each potato and bake on an oven shelf for about 1 hour until the skins are crisp and the insides soft. Serve the pork and beans with the baked potatoes.

**Per serving** 1659kJ/395kcal (20%), 11.8g fat (17%), 3.6g saturates (18%), 10.1g sugars (11%), 1.55g salt (26%)

# Toad in the hole with onion gravy

A classic combination. This gravy is great with toad in the hole, but also with grilled chops, mashed potato or your favourite sausages

**FOR THE TOAD IN THE HOLE**
115g plain flour
freshly ground black pepper
2 medium eggs, beaten, plus
1 egg white
180ml semi-skimmed milk
½ tsp dried sage
½ tsp English mustard
2 tbsp sunflower oil

454g pack Be good to yourself
Cumberland pork sausages by
Sainsbury's

**FOR THE ONION GRAVY**
½ tbsp olive oil
1 onion, finely sliced
1 tbsp Fairtrade light brown
soft sugar by Sainsbury's

2 tbsp plain flour
300ml vegetable stock
(made with ½ reduced salt
stock cube and boiling water)
1 tsp wholegrain mustard, plus
extra to serve (optional)
2 sprigs fresh thyme, leaves
picked and washed
1 tsp Worcestershire sauce

**1** Preheat the oven to 220°C/200°C fan/gas 7. Sift the flour into a large jug or mixing bowl and season with black pepper. Make a well in the centre and add the beaten eggs and egg white. Whisk in the eggs, gradually drawing in the flour and adding just enough milk to make a paste. When all of the flour has been incorporated, whisk in the remaining milk until the batter is as thick as double cream. Stir in the sage and mustard. Set aside.

**2** In the meantime, start the gravy. Heat the oil in a small, non-stick pan over a medium heat. Add the onion and cook gently for 15 minutes until very soft. Stir in the sugar and cook for another 5 minutes. Stir in the flour, then gradually add the stock, stirring continuously. Bring to the boil and simmer gently for 4 minutes, adding the mustard, thyme and Worcestershire sauce for the last minute. Season to taste.

**3** Meanwhile, put the oil in a 25 x 30 x 7cm heavy-based roasting tin and heat for 5 minutes. Add the sausages and cook in the oven for 15 minutes until the oil is very hot. Space the sausages out evenly in the tin, then carefully pour the batter over. Return to the oven for 20-25 minutes, or until well-risen and golden. Serve with the onion gravy and extra mustard, if you like.

**Per serving** 1916kJ/455kcal (23%), 13.5g fat (19%), 3.2g saturates (16%), 10.8g sugars (12%), 1.97g salt (33%)

 **Get ahead**
Make the batter up to 1 day in advance, cover and refrigerate. Return to room temperature, then follow the recipe from step 2.

# Roasted pork chops with mustard rub

These tasty pork chops are great paired with purple sprouting broccoli and roasted fennel

4 tsp English mustard
by Sainsbury's
a few stalks thyme, leaves
only, washed and finely chopped
a few stalks rosemary, leaves
only, finely chopped
freshly ground black pepper
2 x 450g packs British pork
chops by Sainsbury's, 4 chops
in total, trimmed of fat

2 onions, sliced
2 fennel bulbs, trimmed and
sliced horizontally
1 tbsp olive oil
200g purple sprouting broccoli
or Tenderstem broccoli,
stalks trimmed

1 Preheat the oven to 180ºC/160ºC fan/gas 4. In a bowl, combine the mustard, thyme and rosemary, and season with black pepper. Rub this mixture all over the pork chops and put to one side.

2 Arrange the onions and fennel in a roasting tin, season and drizzle over the olive oil. Add the pork chops, nestling them in amongst the vegetables. Transfer to the oven to cook for about 40 minutes, or until the pork is cooked through with no pink colour remaining and the onions and fennel are starting to caramelize.

3 Meanwhile, add the broccoli to a pan of boiling water and cook for 8-10 minutes, or until tender, then drain. Arrange the pork and roasted vegetables on plates with the broccoli on the side, and serve.

**Per serving** 2570kJ/616kcal (31%), 35.8g fat (51%), 11.9g saturates (60%), 6.9g sugars (8%), 0.88g salt (15%)

**Cook's tip**
Cover the tin with foil if the vegetables are beginning to colour too quickly.

# Easy carbonara

This simple yet delicious dish is ideal for midweek entertaining
- and can be on the table in 20 minutes

100g Italian Parma ham slices
from Sainsbury's deli counter
300g dried long pasta, such as
tagliatelle, spaghetti, linguine
or pappardelle
150ml half-fat crème fraîche
by Sainsbury's

150ml single cream
30g finely grated Parmesan
cheese, plus 10g extra to serve
freshly ground black pepper

1 Preheat the grill on its highest setting. Line an oven tray with foil. Place the slices of Parma ham on the foil-lined tray and grill for 3-4 minutes on one side until crispy. Set aside.

2 Bring a large pan of water to the boil and cook the pasta according to the pack instructions.

3 Drain the pasta and return it to the pan. Crumble over the crispy grilled ham and stir in the crème fraîche, cream and cheese. Season well with black pepper. Serve with extra Parmesan sprinkled on top.

**Per serving** 2131kJ/508kcal (25%), 20.4g fat (29%), 11.6g saturates (58%), 5.4g sugars (6%), 0.79g salt (13%)

# Pork enchiladas

A mix of fabulous flavours: tortilla wraps filled with smoky pork and tomato salsa, baked with cheese and soured cream

400g pork tenderloin fillet, from Sainsbury's meat counter
6 Be good to yourself wraps by Sainsbury's
4 tbsp Be good to yourself soured cream by Sainsbury's, for topping
75g mature Cheddar cheese, grated, for topping
170g bag Italian-style salad by Sainsbury's, to serve

**FOR THE MARINADE**
1 ½ tbsp olive oil
1 jalapeño chilli, deseeded and finely chopped
2 tsp coriander seeds
pinch of ground cinnamon
freshly ground black pepper
pinch of sugar

**FOR THE TOMATO SALSA**
500g vine-ripened tomatoes
1 red chilli, halved and deseeded
1 tbsp olive oil
2 spring onions, trimmed and finely chopped
1 lime, juice only
freshly ground black pepper
handful of fresh coriander leaves, washed and finely chopped

**1** Put the pork in a shallow dish, mix the marinade ingredients and pour over the pork to cover. Cover and leave for 20 minutes, or longer if time permits. Preheat the oven to 200°C/180°C fan/gas 6. Transfer the pork (with the marinade) to a roasting tin and cook for 40 minutes, basting occasionally so the pork doesn't dry out, until it is cooked through with no pink remaining. Remove and set aside.

**2** For the salsa, heat a frying or griddle pan to hot. Toss the tomatoes and chilli with the oil and add to the pan. Cook over a medium-high heat for 5-6 minutes, turning halfway, until lightly coloured. Remove and pulse with the spring onions and lime juice in a food processor or using a hand blender until chopped. Season with black pepper, transfer to a bowl and stir through the coriander.

**3** Shred the pork, retaining any of the juices. Lay out the wraps and spoon the pork into the centre of each. Spoon over the salsa and roll up the wraps. Sit them in an ovenproof dish, spoon the soured cream on top and sprinkle with the cheese. Bake for 15-20 minutes until the cheese has melted. Serve with the remaining salsa.

**Per serving** 2132kJ/508kcal (25%), 20.3g fat (29%), 8.3g saturates (42%), 7.3g sugars (8%), 1.21g salt (20%)

# Pork stir-fry with cashew nuts and greens

This tasty stir-fry is perfect for a speedy midweek meal – it can be on the table in half an hour or less

1 tbsp sunflower oil

1 onion, chopped

2.5cm piece fresh root ginger, peeled and finely chopped

3 garlic cloves, finely chopped

1 red chilli, deseeded and finely sliced

400g pork tenderloin fillet, from Sainsbury's meat counter, finely sliced

3 tbsp soy sauce reduced salt by Sainsbury's

1 tbsp sesame oil

50g unsalted cashew nuts

200g pack pak choi, roughly sliced lengthways

1 lime, cut into wedges, to serve

1 Heat the sunflower oil in a wok or deep frying pan, add the onion and stir-fry quickly for a minute. Add the ginger, garlic and chilli and cook, stirring continually to make sure the ingredients don't burn.

2 Add in the pork, and stir-fry for 3-5 minutes until cooked through with no pink remaining, then add the remaining ingredients and cook for a further 3-5 minutes, stirring occasionally until the pak choi is tender and wilted. Serve immediately with the lime wedges.

**Per serving** 1172kJ/280kcal (14%), 15.2g fat (22%), 3.2g saturates (16%), 4.6g sugars (5%), 0.98g salt (16%)

# Pork tenderloin with chillies and tomatoes

This fiery pork dish looks impressive but is simple to make. Serve with a selection of green vegetables

1 jalapeño chilli, deseeded
1 tbsp capucine capers by Sainsbury's, rinsed
8 large sun-dried antipasto tomatoes in oil by Sainsbury's, drained
450g pork tenderloin fillet, from Sainsbury's meat counter

1 tbsp olive oil
freshly ground black pepper
450g pack green vegetable selection by Sainsbury's, cooked according to pack instructions, to serve

**1** Preheat the oven to 200°C/180°C fan/gas 6. Put the jalapeño, capers and sun-dried tomatoes in a food processor or blender and process to form a paste.

**2** Slice the pork along its length, making sure that you don't cut all the way through it. Rub with the oil and season with black pepper.

**3** Stuff the paste into the slit in the pork, spreading it evenly. Pull the edges of the pork up around the stuffing and transfer the meat to a roasting tin, cut-side down. Roast the pork for 30-35 minutes, or until it is cooked through with no pink remaining. Allow the meat to rest for 5 minutes before slicing, then serve with the green vegetables.

**Per serving** 1362kJ/327kcal (16%), 18.7g fat (27%), 4.5g saturates (23%), 4.4g sugars (5%), 0.54g salt (9%)

# Quiche Lorraine

Named after the Lorraine region of north-east France, this classic egg and bacon flan is the original quiche

**FOR THE PASTRY**
200g plain flour, plus extra
for dusting
100g baking block, cubed
1 egg yolk, beaten with 2 tbsp
chilled water

**FOR THE FILLING**
200g pack Be good to yourself
smoked bacon medallions by
Sainsbury's, chopped

1 onion, finely chopped
70g Gruyère cheese, grated
4 medium eggs, lightly beaten
150ml single cream
150ml semi-skimmed milk
freshly ground black pepper

**TO SERVE**
70g bag wild rocket leaves
by Sainsbury's

1 To make the pastry, put the flour and baking block in a large bowl and rub with your fingertips until the mixture resembles fine crumbs. Then add the egg yolk and chilled water, and mix to make a smooth dough. Turn the dough out on a floured surface and knead briefly. Wrap in cling film and chill for 30 minutes. Preheat the oven to 190°C/170°C fan/gas 5.

2 On a lightly floured surface, roll out the pastry to about the thickness of a pound coin, and line a 24cm loose-bottomed tart tin with it, pressing it to the sides. Prick the base of the pastry with a fork, and line with greaseproof & non-stick baking paper by Sainsbury's and baking beans. Blind bake for 12 minutes, then remove the paper and beans, and bake for a further 10 minutes, or until it is light golden in colour.

3 Meanwhile, heat a large frying pan and dry-fry the bacon for 3–4 minutes. Add the onion, fry for a further 2–3 minutes, then spread the onion and bacon over the pastry case. Add the cheese.

4 Whisk together the eggs, cream, milk and black pepper, and pour into the pastry case. Place the tin on an oven tray and bake for 25–30 minutes, or until golden and just set. Allow to set, then slice and serve while still hot.

**Per serving** 1429kJ/342kcal (17%), 20.1g fat (29%), 8.6g saturates (43%), 3.6g sugars (4%), 1.2g salt (20%)

**Get ahead**
Cook up to 48 hours in advance, let cool
cover and refrigerate. Reheat in a medium oven.

# Vegetarian

# Split pea, noodle and vegetable pot

The split peas will gradually absorb all the wonderful flavours of the spices, herbs and coconut in this noodle dish

300g pack fresh rice noodles by Sainsbury's
1 tbsp olive oil
1 onion, finely chopped
freshly ground black pepper
3 carrots, diced
2 garlic cloves, finely chopped
2cm piece fresh root ginger, peeled and grated
1 tsp turmeric
1 tsp coriander seeds, crushed

225g yellow split peas, rinsed
200ml coconut milk (made with 50g creamed coconut dissolved in boiling water)
1 litre hot vegetable stock (made with 1 stock cube and boiling water)
2 courgettes, diced
handful of coriander leaves, washed and chopped, to serve

**1** Soak the noodles in boiling water for 5 minutes, or according to pack instructions, then drain and set aside.

**2** Heat the oil in a large, heavy-based pan. Add the onion and cook on a low heat for 2-3 minutes. Season with black pepper. Stir in the carrots, garlic, ginger, turmeric and coriander seeds and cook for 2 minutes.

**3** Stir in the split peas and add the coconut milk. Increase the heat and allow to bubble for 1 minute, then add the stock and bring to the boil.

**4** Reduce to a simmer and cook over a low heat, partially covered, for 40-50 minutes, or until the split peas begin to soften. Top up with hot water as needed – there should be plenty of liquid. Add the courgettes for the last 5 minutes of cooking. Stir in the noodles and heat through for 2 minutes. Serve garnished with the chopped coriander.

**Per serving** 1202kJ/286kcal (14%), 8.7g fat (12%), 3.7g saturates (19%), 10.3g sugars (11%), 1.67g salt (28%)

# Brazilian black bean and butternut squash stew

This unusual stew, with a mixture of sweet and savoury ingredients, makes a tasty meal for friends and family

1 tbsp olive oil
1 onion, finely chopped
freshly ground black pepper
3 garlic cloves, finely chopped
1 small butternut squash, peeled, deseeded and diced
2 red peppers, deseeded and diced
2 x 390g cartons chopped tomatoes by Sainsbury's
1 small green chilli, deseeded and diced

2 x 380g cartons SO Organic black beans by Sainsbury's, drained and rinsed
500ml vegetable stock (made from 1 stock cube and boiling water)
1 mango, peeled, stoned and diced
bunch of fresh coriander, washed and chopped

**TO SERVE**
3 tbsp Be good to yourself soured cream by Sainsbury's
350g basmati rice, cooked according to pack instructions

1 Preheat the oven to 200°C/180°C fan/gas 6. Heat the oil in a large heavy-based pan over a medium heat, add the onion and cook for 3-4 minutes until soft. Season with black pepper, then stir in the garlic, and cook for 1-2 minutes until soft. Stir in the butternut squash, red peppers, tomatoes and chilli.

2 Add the beans, pour in the stock and bring to a brisk simmer. Then reduce to a gentle simmer, cover with the lid and put in the oven for 50 minutes. Taste and season with black pepper, if necessary, then stir in the mango and coriander. Serve with some soured cream and rice on the side.

**Per serving** 1983kJ/470kcal (24%), 5.5g fat (8%), 1.9g saturates (10%), 18.0g sugars (20%), 1.01g salt (17%)

# Thai red vegetable curry

This versatile curry can be easily adapted to embrace the best seasonal produce. Aubergine and peppers are featured here but squashes would also be delicious

2 tbsp Thai red curry paste by Sainsbury's
400ml tin coconut milk light by Sainsbury's
2 aubergines, cut into chunks
1 red pepper, deseeded and cut into strips
1 green pepper, deseeded and cut into strips
6 kaffir lime leaves, torn in half lengthways
300ml vegetable stock (made with ¹/₂ reduced salt stock cube and boiling water)

1 tbsp palm sugar or Fairtrade demerara cane sugar by Sainsbury's
splash of soy sauce reduced salt by Sainsbury's
1 lime, juice only
handful of fresh coriander, washed and chopped

**TO SERVE**
250g Thai sticky rice by Sainsbury's, cooked according to pack instructions
1 lime, cut into wedges

**1** Heat the curry paste in a large frying pan or wok over a medium-high heat for a few seconds, stirring around the pan. Shake the tin of coconut milk, then pour into the pan or wok. Bring to a gentle boil, stirring occasionally, and cook for 2–3 minutes until the sauce releases its aroma.

**2** Add the aubergines, peppers, lime leaves, stock, sugar and soy sauce. Bring to the boil again. Reduce the heat slightly and simmer gently for about 15 minutes until the vegetables are soft.

**3** Now add the lime juice and stir well. Taste and adjust the seasoning accordingly, adding more sugar (sweetness), or lime juice (sourness). Stir in the coriander and serve immediately with the sticky rice and the lime wedges to squeeze over.

**Per serving** 1573kJ/376kcal (19%), 8.6g fat (12%), 5.8g saturates (29%), 13.6g sugars (15%), 1.62g salt (27%)

# Butternut squash tagine

Serve this vegetarian-friendly tagine with fluffy couscous for a delicious, spicy meal

2½ tbsp olive oil
2 red onions, finely chopped
1 large red pepper, cut into large pieces
4 garlic cloves, chopped
5cm piece fresh root ginger, peeled and finely chopped
1 tsp chilli powder
1 tsp ground cinnamon
2 tsp smoked paprika
2 tsp ground coriander
1 tbsp ground cumin
2 x 390g cartons chopped tomatoes
600ml vegetable stock (made with 1 stock cube and boiling water)

1 tbsp clear honey
freshly ground black pepper
400g butternut squash, peeled, deseeded and cut into cubes
400g tin chickpeas by Sainsbury's, drained and rinsed
75g dried apricots, chopped
bunch of fresh coriander leaves, washed and chopped
freshly ground black pepper
160g couscous, cooked according to pack instructions, to serve

1 Pour the oil into a large pan. Add the onions, red pepper, garlic and ginger, and fry over a low heat, stirring, for 2 minutes until they are just beginning to soften, but not brown.

2 Add the chilli, cinnamon, smoked paprika, ground coriander and ground cumin, and continue to cook for another 2 minutes over a low heat to release all the flavours of the spices. Add the tomatoes, stock and honey, stir to combine and season with black pepper. Increase the heat to bring the sauce to the boil, then stir and reduce the heat once more. Simmer slowly, uncovered, for 30 minutes.

3 Add the butternut squash, chickpeas and dried apricots and continue to cook for 10-15 minutes until the squash is just soft but the pieces are not falling apart. Add a little more water if it is beginning to look a little dry. Season with black pepper and stir in the coriander leaves before serving. Serve the tagine on a bed of couscous.

**Per serving** 1914kJ/455kcal (23%), 10.6g fat (15%), 1.9g saturates (10%), 32.7g sugars (36%), 1.56g salt (26%)

# Mixed vegetable tagine

One of the ingredients that gives a Moroccan tagine its unique flavour is preserved lemon, a traditional taste of the region

1 tbsp olive oil
1 red onion, roughly chopped
freshly ground black pepper
3 garlic cloves, finely chopped
5cm piece fresh root ginger, peeled and grated
1 tsp ground turmeric
pinch of saffron threads
1 tsp coriander seeds, ground
½ tsp cumin seeds
4 large potatoes, peeled and chopped into chunks
3 carrots, peeled and chopped into chunks
1 fennel bulb, trimmed and chopped into chunks

4 tomatoes, finely chopped
750ml vegetable stock (made with 1 stock cube and boiling water)
handful of mixed olives, stoned and halved (optional)
8 slices preserved lemon by Sainsbury's, flesh removed and peel chopped
bunch of fresh coriander leaves, washed and roughly chopped
250g couscous, cooked according to pack instructions, to serve

1 Heat the oil in a large heavy-based pan over a medium heat, add the onion and cook for 3-4 minutes until soft. Season with black pepper, stir through the garlic, ginger, turmeric, saffron, coriander seeds and cumin, and cook for a couple of minutes.

2 Add the potatoes and toss to coat, then add the carrots and fennel and stir so everything is well combined. Cook for a few minutes, add the tomatoes and pour over just enough hot stock to cover the vegetables.

3 Partially cover with the lid and simmer very gently for 30-40 minutes until the vegetables are soft and a lot of the liquid has evaporated. Top up with more hot stock if needed. Taste and season with black pepper, then stir through the olives and lemon and half the coriander leaves. Transfer to a serving dish and sprinkle over the remaining coriander leaves. Serve with couscous.

**Per serving** 1134kJ/269kcal (14%), 4.8g fat (7%), 0.8g saturates (4%), 8.3g sugars (9%), 1.07g salt (18%)

**SERVES** 4
**PREP** 10 minutes
**COOK** 20 minutes

# Pasta primavera

This delicate sauce is an easy and delicious way to get green vegetables into your family's diet

100g sugarsnap peas

125g fine asparagus spears, halved

100g baby courgettes, quartered lengthways

400g dried linguine by Sainsbury's

1 tbsp olive oil

2 garlic cloves, finely sliced

1 shallot, finely chopped

1 tbsp extra virgin olive oil

100ml half-fat crème fraîche by Sainsbury's

½ tsp grated nutmeg

1 lemon, finely grated zest plus juice of ½ lemon

2 tbsp torn basil leaves, washed

2 tbsp chopped flat-leaf parsley leaves, washed

freshly ground black pepper

100g bag young leaf spinach

15g Basics Italian hard cheese by Sainsbury's, shaved, to serve

**1** Bring a large pan of water to the boil and add the sugarsnap peas, asparagus and courgettes. Return to the boil and cook for 3 minutes, or until the vegetables are just tender, but still brightly coloured and al dente. Drain well, then run under cold water to set the colour. Drain once more, and set aside in the colander over the kitchen sink.

**2** Refill the pan used for cooking the vegetables with more water and bring it to the boil. Cook the pasta according to the pack instructions. Meanwhile, heat the olive oil in a small pan over a medium heat and sauté the garlic and shallot for 2 minutes.

**3** In a medium jug, combine the extra virgin olive oil, crème fraîche, nutmeg, lemon zest and juice, basil and parsley. Add the cooked garlic and shallot. Stir well and season with black pepper.

**4** Drain the pasta well in the same colander as the vegetables, to reheat them slightly, then return the pasta and vegetables to the pan. Add the spinach and stir until it wilts. Add the herb sauce to the pasta and stir to coat.

**5** Transfer to warm serving bowls and serve topped with shavings of Italian hard cheese.

**Per serving** 2117kJ/502kcal (25%), 12.1g fat (17%), 5g saturates (25%), 7.1g sugars (8%), 0.37g salt (6%)

**Get ahead**
The herb sauce can be prepared up to 1 day in advance, covered and kept in the fridge until needed. Whisk it once more to emulsify before use.

# Vegetable lasagne

This is a delicious vegetarian version of the Italian classic, with a speedy substitute for the traditional béchamel sauce

2 tbsp olive oil
2 red onions, roughly chopped
1 aubergine, cut into 3cm cubes
1 red pepper, deseeded and cut into 3cm pieces
1 yellow pepper, deseeded and cut into 3cm pieces
1 courgette, cut into 3cm cubes
1 fennel bulb, finely sliced
3 garlic cloves, roughly chopped
1 tsp dried rosemary
1 tsp dried basil
freshly ground black pepper
500ml carton tomato passata by Sainsbury's

200ml half-fat crème fraîche
200ml low-fat natural yogurt
2 eggs, beaten
60g Basics Italian hard cheese by Sainsbury's, finely grated
250g pack fresh lasagne sheets by Sainsbury's
100g Be good to yourself mozzarella cheese by Sainsbury's, torn into pieces
2 x 170g bags Italian style salad by Sainsbury's, to serve

**1** Preheat the oven to 200°C/180°C fan/gas 6. Pour the oil into a large roasting tin and heat in the oven for 5 minutes.

**2** Add all the vegetables to the tin with the garlic, herbs and plenty of black pepper. Stir well and return the tin to the oven for 30 minutes, stirring occasionally. Remove, then stir the passata into the roasted vegetables.

**3** Meanwhile, place the crème fraîche, yogurt, eggs and hard cheese in a jug, season with black pepper and whisk together with a fork. Place half the vegetables in the base of a 28 x 29 x 5cm ovenproof dish and top with half the lasagne. Repeat the layers.

**4** Pour the egg mixture over the lasagne and top with the mozzarella cheese. Place the dish on an oven tray and bake for 30 minutes. Serve with the salad on the side.

**Per serving** 1474kJ/352kcal (18%), 16.7g fat (24%), 7.8g saturates (39%), 15.9g sugars (18%), 0.8g salt (13%)

# Butternut squash, spinach and goat's cheese frittata

Fritatta is an egg-based dish from Italy, where the name translates as 'fried'. This vegetarian one is equally good with chopped Swiss chard or pak choi instead of the spinach

1 small butternut squash (about 500g), peeled, halved, deseeded and diced

2 tbsp olive oil

10g unsalted butter

1 small onion, chopped

260g bag young spinach

150g pot mild French goat's cheese

4 pieces of sun-dried tomatoes in oil by Sainsbury's, drained and cut into small pieces

2 tbsp Basics Italian hard cheese by Sainsbury's, grated

grated nutmeg

2 tbsp chopped tarragon

6 medium eggs, beaten

freshly ground black pepper

1 Blanch the squash in boiling water for 2-4 minutes to soften slightly. Drain thoroughly.

2 Heat the oil and butter in a large ovenproof frying pan. Add the onion and fry, stirring, for 3 minutes until softened and lightly golden. Add the squash and fry, stirring, for 2 minutes until tender, but still holding its shape.

3 Scatter the spinach into the pan and cook, stirring, for 2 minutes to wilt. Cook for 1-2 minutes to allow any liquid to evaporate, stirring gently and spreading the spinach evenly into the squash. Add small spoonfuls or pieces of the goat's cheese and sun-dried tomatoes. Sprinkle with cheese, dust with nutmeg and scatter the tarragon over.

4 Season the beaten eggs with black pepper. Pour into the pan and cook, lifting and stirring, until beginning to set. Cover the pan and cook gently for about 5 minutes until the eggs are almost set and the base is golden.

5 Meanwhile, preheat the grill. When the eggs are nearly set, put the pan under the grill for about 3 minutes to finish setting - the frittata should only just be starting to colour so that all the colours remain vibrant. Remove from the grill and leave to cool for at least 5 minutes. Serve warm or cold, cut into wedges.

**Per serving** 964kJ/232kcal (12%), 14.7g fat (21%), 5.0g saturates (25%), 5.8g sugars (6%), 0.61g salt (10%)

# Bulgur wheat with mixed peppers, mint and goat's cheese

This tasty salad is simple to prepare and is great for picnics or a packed lunch for work

250g cracked bulgur wheat by Sainsbury's
300ml vegetable stock (made with ½ stock cube and boiling water)
freshly ground black pepper
165g bunch of spring onions, finely chopped
1 orange pepper, deseeded and diced
1 yellow pepper, deseeded and diced

pinch of paprika
handful of fresh mint leaves, washed and finely chopped
1 lemon, juice only
125g Taste the Difference French goat's cheese by Sainsbury's, crumbled
½ tbsp extra virgin olive oil, for drizzling

1 Put the bulgur wheat in a large bowl, and pour over the stock – it should just cover the bulgur. Stir well and cover with an upturned plate, then leave to stand for 10 minutes. Stir with a fork to fluff up the grains, and season with black pepper.

2 Add the spring onions, orange and yellow peppers, paprika, mint and lemon juice, and stir well. Taste and season with black pepper, if necessary.

3 To serve, top with the goat's cheese and a drizzle of olive oil.

**Per serving** 914kJ/218kcal (11%), 9.3g fat (13%), 5.6g saturates (28%), 6.2g sugars (7%), 0.99g salt (17%)

**Why not try?**
Use skinned, chopped tomatoes, instead of the peppers.

**SERVES** 4
**PREP** 20 minutes
**COOK** 40 minutes,
plus resting

# Sweet potato, spinach and feta tortilla

This vegetarian dish can be served for breakfast, lunch or even cold for a picnic as it's so easy to transport

200g sweet potatoes, peeled and cut into 1cm cubes

2 tbsp olive oil

100g bag young leaf spinach

6 eggs

1 tbsp half-fat crème fraîche by Sainsbury's

freshly ground black pepper

75g Greek feta cheese by Sainsbury's, crumbled

1 Preheat the oven to 190°C/170°C fan/gas 5. Toss the sweet potatoes in ½ tablespoon of the oil, space out on a baking tray and roast for 15-20 minutes until cooked through and golden at the edges.

2 Heat ½ tablespoon of the oil in a 25cm non-stick, ovenproof frying pan. Add the spinach and cook over a high heat for 2 minutes until it wilts. When the spinach is cool enough to handle, squeeze it well to drain off excess moisture, then chop it up.

3 Whisk together the eggs and crème fraîche in a large bowl and season generously with black pepper. Add the sweet potato, spinach and feta and mix well.

4 Heat the remaining oil in the pan over a medium heat and pour in the egg mixture. Cook for 5 minutes, without moving it, until the edges start to set.

5 Transfer the pan to the oven and cook for a further 10 minutes until the tortilla is set and golden on top. Rest for at least 5 minutes before cutting into wedges to serve warm or at room temperature.

**Per serving** 1132kJ/272kcal (14%), 17.6g fat (25%), 6.4g saturates (32%), 3.5g sugars (4%), 0.77g salt (13%)

# Spiced lemon lentils with roast potatoes

This dish uses Puy lentils, named after the region in France where they are grown. Here they're combined with chickpeas and potatoes to make a delicious meal

175g Puy lentils, rinsed and any grit removed
900ml vegetable stock (made with 1 stock cube and boiling water)
freshly ground black pepper
3 Maris Piper potatoes, peeled and cut into 2.5cm cubes
2 tbsp olive oil
2 red chillies, deseeded and finely chopped

2 tsp cumin seeds
2 garlic cloves, finely chopped
1 lemon, zest and juice
1 onion, finely chopped
1 red pepper, deseeded and finely chopped
400g tin chickpeas by Sainsbury's, drained and rinsed
1 tbsp flat-leaf parsley, washed and finely chopped

**TO SERVE**
2 x 100g bags watercress, spinach and rocket salad by Sainsbury's

**1** Preheat the oven to 200°C/180°C fan/gas 6. Put the lentils in a large pan and cover with the stock. Season well with black pepper and bring to the boil, remove any foam on the surface of the liquid and then simmer gently for 20–25 minutes, or until the lentils are soft. If the lentils look as if they are drying out, top up with a little more stock. Drain and set aside.

**2** While the lentils are cooking, toss the potatoes in 1 tablespoon of the olive oil and put them in a large roasting tin along with the chillies and cumin seeds. Season well with black pepper. Roast in the oven for 30–35 minutes, giving them a shake or a stir halfway through, and add the garlic and lemon zest at the same time.

**3** Heat the remaining oil in a large, heavy-based, deep frying pan. Add the onion and red pepper, and cook for about 5 minutes, or until the pepper softens. Tip in the chickpeas and the cooked lentils, stir well and then stir in the lemon juice and parsley. If you prefer a wetter mixture, add a little hot stock and let it cook for a few minutes. Serve topped with a spoonful of the roast potatoes and a green salad.

**Per serving** 1712kJ/406kcal (20%), 8.6g fat (12%), 1.4g saturates (7%), 7.0g sugars (8%), 1.17g salt (20%)

# Fiery pepper noodles

A wonderfully spicy vegetarian dish, where the lime and chilli work well with the crunchy peanut butter

1 red pepper, whole

1 green pepper, whole

1 tbsp sunflower oil

4 spring onions, chopped

1 garlic clove, finely chopped

1 courgette, finely chopped

2 green jalapeño chillies, deseeded and chopped

2cm fresh root ginger, peeled and grated

1 tbsp chopped flat-leaf parsley leaves

1 tbsp chopped coriander leaves, plus a few torn leaves, washed, to serve

1 lime, zest and juice

4 tbsp crunchy peanut butter by Sainsbury's

3 tbsp soy sauce reduced salt by Sainsbury's

1 tbsp dry sherry

410g pack free-range fresh egg noodles by Sainsbury's

1  Preheat the oven to 200°C/180°C fan/gas 6. Put the peppers in a roasting tin and cook for 25-30 minutes until they begin to char. Remove from the oven, put in a plastic bag and leave to cool before removing the stalks and skin, deseeding and roughly chopping. (Take care, as the juices inside will be hot.)

2 Heat the oil in a wok or large frying pan over a high heat. Add the spring onions, garlic and courgette, and stir-fry for 1 minute, constantly moving the ingredients so they do not catch and burn on the pan. Add the peppers, chillies, ginger, herbs, lime zest and juice, peanut butter, soy sauce, sherry and add up to 120ml water. Stir until the peanut butter melts into the rest of the sauce.

3 Add the noodles and toss for 2 minutes, or until piping hot throughout. Pile into warm bowls and sprinkle with the torn coriander leaves to serve.

**Per serving** 1203kJ/287kcal (14%), 11.5g fat (16%), 1.8g saturates (9%), 6.3g sugars (7%), 0.09g salt (2%)

# Butternut squash and spinach curry

This aromatic curry pairs soft butternut squash with fresh spinach for a colourful meal that's full of flavour

1 tbsp vegetable oil
1 large onion, chopped
1 medium butternut squash, about 1.25kg, peeled, deseeded and cut into 2cm cubes
2 garlic cloves, crushed
2-3 tbsp rogan josh curry paste by Sainsbury's
390g carton chopped tomatoes
360ml vegetable stock (made with ½ stock cube and boiling water)

260g bag young spinach by Sainsbury's
freshly ground black pepper

**TO SERVE**
360g basmati rice by Sainsbury's, cooked according to pack instructions
3 tbsp low-fat natural yogurt by Sainsbury's

**1** Heat the oil in a large, deep pan, add the onion and cook gently for 2-3 minutes. Add the butternut squash, garlic and curry paste and cook for a further 2-3 minutes.

**2** Add the tomatoes and stock. Bring to the boil, then reduce the heat, cover and simmer for 15 minutes, stirring occasionally. Remove the lid and simmer for a further 10 minutes. Add a little extra stock or water if it becomes too dry.

**3** Stir in the spinach, cover and cook for 1-2 minutes until just wilted. Season with black pepper and spoon into serving bowls. Serve with the rice and a spoonful of yogurt on top.

**Per serving** 1545kJ/366 kcal (18%), 4.8g fat (7%), 0.9g saturates (5%), 10.8g sugars (12%), 0.61g salt (10%)

# Rice

**^ Arborio** and **Italian carnaroli** are premium short grain rices used for making risotto. Both varieties are high in starch, which helps give the classic dish its characteristic creamy texture. Carnaroli has a higher starch content and longer grain than arborio.

**^ Basmati rice** is a long grain variety grown in the Himalayan foothills of India and Pakistan. It is matured to reduce its moisture content and enhance its fragrance and flavour. Available in white or brown form, basmati is ideal for using in pilafs or serving with curries.

**< Paella** rice, like arborio and carnaroli, absorbs the flavours of the other ingredients through gradual cooking; paella rice can absorb up to three times its volume in liquid. Once cooked, the short grains will become sticky but remain distinct and 'al dente'.

**^ Basmati and wild** rice are a great combination; plain, nutty basmati provides a base for the intense, tea-like flavour of wild rice, which is actually a grass and not a rice. Great in pilafs, salads or stuffings.

**< Pudding** rice is a short grain white rice that becomes soft and creamy when cooked in sweetened milk to make rice pudding. Like risotto rices and paella rice, pudding rice will absorb the flavours of the liquid it is cooked in.

< **Thai fragrant** rice is a slightly sticky long grain variety with a delicious, floral aroma. It is commonly used to accompany Thai and Chinese savoury dishes.

^ **Thai sticky** rice becomes sticky on cooking, so that the grains adhere when lightly pressed together. Best cooked by steaming so that the grains remain distinct. Serve with Thai dishes.

^ **French Camargue red** rice is a speciality crop grown in the wetlands of the Camargue region of southern France. A nutty-tasting rice with a visually appealing red grain coat. Good for salads and side dishes.

^ **Long grain** rice is the most versatile variety to use for side dishes, salads and pilafs, thanks to an unobtrusive, sweet flavour that marries well with most cuisines. Available as white or brown rice, the latter undergoing minimal milling, which gives it its slightly chewy texture.

^ **Thai black** rice has dark purple grains with a fruity, grassy aroma. Most commonly served as a sweet breakfast cereal, a dumpling-like snack or a pudding flavoured with coconut milk and palm sugar.

## No time to cook?

Easy cook and microwave rices are also available – perfect if you're short on time. Easy cook rice is steamed under pressure with the husk on after harvesting; this helps the grains remain separate, but still fluffy, once they're cooked. Both brown and white varieties are available. Microwave rice can be bought frozen or vacuum-packed, plain and pre-seasoned, in a number of rice varieties.

# Cinnamon, almond and raisin brown rice pilaf with griddled aubergine

There's a real taste of the Middle East in this sweet-spiced pilaf.
White rice can also be used, but cook it for 20 minutes only

1 tbsp sunflower oil, plus
extra for brushing
2 celery sticks, chopped
1 leek, chopped
2 carrots, peeled and chopped
1 garlic clove, crushed
225g brown basmati rice
1 tsp ground cinnamon
2cm fresh ginger, peeled
and grated

½ tsp ground cumin
1 tsp dried oregano
750ml vegetable stock
(made with ½ stock cube
and boiling water)
4 tbsp raisins by Sainsbury's
115g chestnut mushrooms, sliced
50g whole blanched almonds
freshly ground black pepper

2 aubergines, trimmed and
cut into 5mm thick slices
100g Greek feta cheese
by Sainsbury's, diced
a few sliced black and
green olives, to garnish

**1** Heat the oil in a large saucepan. Add the celery, leek, carrots and garlic and fry, stirring, for 3 minutes. Stir in the rice and spices and cook, stirring, until every grain is glistening.

**2** Add the oregano, stock, raisins, mushrooms, almonds and black pepper. Bring to the boil, stirring, then reduce the heat to low. Cover and cook for 40 minutes, then remove from the heat and leave to stand for 5 minutes.

**3** While the rice is cooking, heat a heavy-based frying pan or griddle pan. Brush the aubergine slices with oil and griddle in batches for 2–3 minutes on each side, pressing down with a fish slice as they cook, until golden and tender. Cover, set aside and keep warm.

**4** Fluff up the rice, taste and adjust the seasoning, if necessary. Gently stir in the aubergine slices and feta, pile onto warm plates and garnish with a few sliced olives.

**Per serving** 1360kJ/326kcal (16%), 19.2g fat (27%), 5.8g saturates (29%), 11.4g sugars (13%), 1.27g salt (21%)

# Stuffed mushrooms en croûte

Chestnuts make a flavourful filling for mushrooms and the creamy sauce adds a tasty finishing touch

1 tbsp olive oil

1 onion, finely chopped

1 celery stick, finely chopped

200g box whole cooked chestnuts, chopped

2 tbsp chopped flat-leaf parsley

2 tbsp chopped thyme

1 lemon, grated zest

2 tbsp mushroom ketchup or Worcestershire sauce

60g fresh wholemeal breadcrumbs

freshly ground black pepper

250g pack large flat mushrooms, wiped and stalks removed

375g pack ready rolled light puff pastry by Sainsbury's

1 egg, beaten

2 x 300g pack dwarf beans by Sainsbury's, cooked according to pack instructions

**FOR THE SAUCE**

1 tbsp sunflower oil

175g chestnut mushrooms, finely chopped

1 garlic clove, crushed

150ml Original Somerset cider by Sainsbury's

1 tbsp plain flour

2 tbsp single cream

2 tsp chopped thyme

1 Heat the oil in a saucepan. Add the onion and celery and fry, stirring, for 3 minutes until softened and lightly golden. Remove from the heat, and add the chestnuts, herbs, lemon zest, ketchup or Worcestershire sauce, breadcrumbs and black pepper. Press the mixture into the inside of the mushrooms.

2 Preheat the oven to 200°C/180°C fan/gas 6. Cut the pastry into rounds about 2cm larger in diameter than the mushrooms. Line a baking sheet with greaseproof & non-stick baking paper by Sainsbury's, lay the rounds on it and place a stuffed mushroom, stuffing side down, in the centre of each. Brush the edges with the beaten egg.

3 Cut the remaining pastry to rounds about 8cm larger than the mushrooms. Place the pastry over and press the edges to seal. Flute the edges with the back of a knife, then brush all over with beaten egg. Make a hole in the centre of each to allow steam to escape. Make leaves out of pastry trimmings, if liked, and arrange on top. Brush with the remaining egg. Bake in the oven for 40 minutes, or until the pastry is puffy and golden and the mushrooms are cooked through.

4 Meanwhile, make the sauce. Heat the sunflower oil in a saucepan and add the chestnut mushrooms, finely chopped mushroom stalks and garlic. Cook, stirring, over a medium heat for about 3 minutes until tender and the liquid has evaporated.

5 Add the cider and boil for 2 minutes until reduced by half. Stir in the flour and cook for 1 minute, then the cream, thyme and 200ml water. Simmer for 3 minutes until reduced and thickened, stirring. Season with black pepper. Transfer the pies to plates and serve with the sauce and green beans.

**Per serving** 2636kJ/629kcal (32%), 24.8g fat (35%), 9.1g saturates (46%), 14.2g sugars (16%), 1.08g salt (18%)

# Beetroot, courgette and goat's cheese pizzas

Buying a pizza base and putting on your own choice of topping means all the family get to eat their favourites. Try this delicious goat's cheese and vegetable option

1 tbsp olive oil
4 small courgettes, sliced
1 red onion, halved and
thinly sliced
1 large garlic clove,
finely chopped
2 tbsp chopped rosemary
150ml passata by Sainsbury's
2 tbsp tomato purée

1 pack stonebaked pizza
bases by Sainsbury's
3 cooked beetroots from
beetroot vacuum pack by
Sainsbury's, diced
110g bag wild rocket, washed
3/4 x 200g goat's cheese log by
Sainsbury's, sliced
freshly ground black pepper

**1** Heat 1 tablespoon of oil in a frying pan. Add the courgettes, onion, garlic and rosemary, and cook, stirring, for 3 minutes until softened but not browned. Set aside.

**2** Preheat the oven to 220°C/200°C fan/gas 7.

**3** Mix the passata with the tomato purée and spread the tomato mixture over the pizza bases, followed by the courgette and onion mixture. Scatter with the beetroot and most of the rocket, then arrange the goat's cheese slices on top. Season with black pepper.

**4** Place the pizzas directly on the top shelf of the oven and place a baking tray on the shelf below. Bake in the oven for 10 minutes until the crust is golden, the cheese is melting, and everything is piping hot.

**5** Remove from the oven and top with the remaining rocket. Cut each pizza in half before serving.

**Per serving** 1792kJ/427kcal (21%), 14.9g fat (21%), 6.6g saturates (33%), 11.6g sugars (13%), 1.19g salt (20%)

**Why not try?**
Try this with peppers instead of courgettes and slices of Camembert for a variation on goat's cheese.

SERVES 4
PREP 20 minutes
COOK 1 hour 15 minutes–
1 hour 30 minutes

# Kitchen garden pie

For a meat-free dish, try cooking up the best your garden has to offer in this delicious potato-topped pie. The types of vegetables used can be varied according to the season

**FOR THE FILLING**
175g pack baby leeks, trimmed, washed and sliced
200g parsnips, peeled and chopped into bite-sized pieces
300g butternut squash, peeled, deseeded and chopped into bite-sized pieces
200g Chantenay carrots, chopped into bite-sized pieces
1 red onion, finely chopped
2 garlic cloves, finely chopped
1 tbsp olive oil

½ tsp dried red chilli flakes
2 tbsp fresh rosemary, chopped, or 1 tsp dried rosemary
freshly ground black pepper
small bunch of curly parsley, stalks removed
50g white breadcrumbs
30g Basics Italian hard cheese by Sainsbury's, grated
1 lemon, grated zest
50g sunflower spread
50g plain flour
450ml semi-skimmed milk

½ tsp English mustard powder
60g mature Cheddar cheese, grated

**FOR THE TOPPING**
1kg Maris Piper or King Edward potatoes, peeled and cut into chunks
25g sunflower spread
30ml semi-skimmed milk
freshly ground black pepper

**1** Preheat the oven to 200°C/180°C fan/gas 6. Place the leeks, parsnips, squash, carrots, onion and garlic in a large roasting tin. Add the olive oil, chilli flakes and rosemary, season with black pepper and toss to coat the vegetables. Roast for 35–45 minutes, or until the vegetables are tender.

**2** To make the topping, cook the potatoes in a saucepan of boiling water for 15 minutes, or until tender. Drain and mash, and stir in the sunflower spread and milk. Mix well to combine, season with black pepper, cover and set aside.

**3** Place the parsley, bread and Italian cheese in a food processor, and pulse to form fine crumbs. Season with black pepper, and stir in the lemon zest.

**4** Melt the sunflower spread in a medium pan. Stir in the flour and cook for 2–3 minutes over a medium heat, stirring constantly with a wooden spoon, until a smooth paste is formed. Gradually add the milk, stirring constantly, to make a white sauce. Stir in the mustard powder, Cheddar cheese and roasted vegetables, and season with black pepper.

**5** Transfer to the ovenproof dish. Top with the mash, spreading it in an even layer and sprinkle over the breadcrumb mixture. Place the dish on a baking tray and bake for 20 minutes. Serve hot.

**Per serving** 2905kJ/692kcal (35%), 25.3g fat (36%), 9.4g saturates (47%), 20.5g sugars (23%), 1.21g salt (20%)

# Side dishes

# Roasted root vegetables

Most root vegetables become sweeter when roasted and can be a delicious alternative to simple roast potatoes

1kg mixed root vegetables, such as Maris Piper potatoes, carrots, parsnips or butternut squash, cut into large wedges
1 large red onion, cut into wedges

2 tbsp olive oil
handful of mixed fresh herb leaves, such as parsley, sage and thyme, finely chopped
freshly ground black pepper

1 Preheat the oven to 200°C/180°C fan/gas 6. Mix all the vegetables, the oil and herbs, and season with black pepper.

2 Arrange in a single layer in a large roasting tin and roast at the top of the oven for 45-55 minutes, turning occasionally, until slightly caramelized at the edges and cooked through. Serve hot.

**Per serving** 885kJ/211kcal (11%), 6.2g fat (9%), 0.9g saturates (5%), 13.5g sugars (15%), 0.07g salt (1%)

# Cabbages and greens

< **Green cabbage** is available in numerous varieties that are great all-rounders. Particularly good steamed or boiled, these are also delicious shredded and added to stir-fries.

^ **Red cabbage** can be used finely shredded and braised, pickled or marinated as a salad. It turns a lovely bright red when used with vinegar, lemon juice or wine.

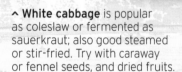

^ **White cabbage** is popular as coleslaw or fermented as sauerkraut; also good steamed or stir-fried. Try with caraway or fennel seeds, and dried fruits.

> **Sweetheart cabbage** is delicious shredded in soups, stews, stir-fries and casseroles, or very finely shredded and deep-fried for a few seconds to make crispy 'seaweed'.

**< Savoy cabbage** is a crinkly-leaved variety with a sweet heart and tender leaves that are best shredded then lightly steamed, boiled or stir-fried. The outer leaves are good stuffed.

**> Kale** has tight, curly, dark green leaves with an intense flavour. Cut out any tough fibrous stalks first. Use fresh, as it can turn bitter if stored for too long.

**^ Spinach** is great wilted as a vegetable or added to stir-fries, soups and stews; baby leaves are delicious in salads. Particularly good flavoured with nutmeg.

**< Cavolo nero**, also known as Tuscan black cabbage, has dark, coarse leaves that should be crisp and straight. Most commonly used in pastas and soups, it goes well with tomatoes, garlic and olives.

**^ Choi sum** is similar to pak choi, with tender, crunchy stalks. It can be used raw in salads, or stir-fried, lightly boiled or steamed.

**^ Pak choi** is a member of the cabbage family and is related to bok choy. It has fleshy stalks and soft leaves. Steam baby ones whole; chop or shred larger ones and stir-fry, or use raw in salads.

# Brussels sprouts with chestnuts and pancetta

A traditional accompaniment to Christmas turkey, this recipe would work well with any roast meal

420g Brussels sprouts, washed and trimmed
½ x 206g pack Italian cubetti di pancetta
10g unsalted butter

100g chestnuts, cooked, peeled and roughly chopped
1 tsp grated lemon zest
freshly ground black pepper

1 Boil the Brussels sprouts in plenty of water for 5-7 minutes, depending on their size, until they are just tender, but not overcooked. Drain them well.

2 In a large frying pan or wok, fry the pancetta in the butter for 3-4 minutes until crispy. Add the Brussels sprouts, chestnuts and lemon zest, and continue to cook for 2 minutes until everything is heated through. Season with black pepper and serve straight away.

**Per serving** 573kJ/138kcal (7%), 8.0g fat (11%), 3.1g saturates (16%), 3.3g sugars (4%), 0.65g salt (11%)

# Braised cauliflower with chilli and coriander

A few spices can turn the humble cauliflower into something far more interesting. This dish can be served as part of an Indian meal, or to spice up a roast

400g cauliflower, outer leaves removed, broken into small florets, smaller inner leaves reserved

2 dried red chillies

1 tsp cumin seeds

1 tbsp sunflower oil

1 tsp mustard seeds by Sainsbury's

½ tsp turmeric

2 garlic cloves, crushed

10g unsalted butter

2 tbsp finely chopped coriander, washed

1 Blanch the cauliflower florets and leaves in boiling water for 1-2 minutes, drain and rinse under cold water.

2 Grind together the chillies and cumin seeds in a mortar and pestle, or with the back of a spoon in a small bowl, until roughly broken down. Heat the sunflower oil in a large, deep-sided frying pan or wok, and add the chilli and cumin seeds, mustard seeds, turmeric and garlic. Cook gently for 1 minute until the mustard seeds start to pop.

3 Add the cauliflower and enough water so that it covers the bottom of the pan (about 6 tablespoons). Bring the water to the boil and cover the pan or wok. Reduce the heat and simmer the cauliflower for 3-5 minutes until almost cooked through.

4 Uncover the pan or wok and turn up the heat. Allow the water to boil away, turning the cauliflower all the time. When all the water has evaporated (about 5-6 minutes), add the butter and mix well until it melts. Sprinkle with coriander before serving hot.

**Per serving** 341kJ/82kcal (4%), 5.5g fat (8%), 1.7g saturates (9%), 2.7g sugars (3%), 0.24g salt (4%)

# Marrow and tomato gratin

Although less sweet than courgettes, marrow becomes more concentrated in flavour when baked. This gratin tastes great with chicken

2 tbsp olive oil

1 onion, finely chopped

900g marrow, halved, deseeded, peeled and cut into cubes

450g tomatoes, finely chopped

3 garlic cloves, grated or finely chopped

handful of fresh flat-leaf parsley, finely chopped

freshly ground black pepper

3 tbsp fresh breadcrumbs

50g Basics Italian hard cheese, grated, plus extra to serve

**1** Preheat the oven to 200°C/180°C fan/gas 6. Heat the oil in a large pan, add the onion and cook over a low heat for 5 minutes, or until soft and translucent. Add the marrow and cook for a further 5 minutes, then add the tomatoes and garlic and cook over a low heat for 10 minutes, or until the tomatoes start to break down. Stir through the parsley and season with black pepper.

**2** Spoon the mixture into 1 large gratin dish or 4 small ones. Sprinkle over the breadcrumbs and cheese and bake in the oven for 20-30 minutes, or until the top is crisp and golden. Sprinkle over a little more cheese then serve.

**Per serving** 765kJ/183kcal (9%), 9.5g fat (14%), 3.1g saturates (16%), 10.6g sugars (12%), 0.30g salt (5%)

**SERVES** 6
**PREP** 20 minutes
**COOK** 1 hour

# Sweet potato and sage gratin

This tasty gratin is delicious served with roast meat or cold ham

300ml half-fat crème fraîche
by Sainsbury's
2 pinches of nutmeg
2 tbsp chopped sage
freshly ground black pepper

25g unsalted butter,
plus extra for greasing
1kg sweet potatoes, peeled
and thinly sliced

1 Preheat the oven to 200°C/180°C fan/gas 6. Whisk the crème fraîche with the nutmeg and sage. Season with black pepper. Grease a 24 x 18cm ovenproof gratin dish with butter and put a layer of sweet potato slices on the bottom. Cover with a layer of the crème fraîche mixture. Repeat until all the sweet potatoes and crème fraîche are used up, ending with a layer of crème fraîche, then dot with butter.

2 Cover with foil and bake for 1 hour, or until completely soft. Serve hot.

**Per serving** 1186kJ/283kcal (14%), 12.2g fat (17%), 7.7g saturates (39%), 11g sugars (12%), 0.28g salt (5%)

SERVES 4
PREP 10 minutes
COOK 35 minutes

# Sweet balsamic onions

Baby onions are also known as pickling onions. Braising them in balsamic vinegar keeps them sweet and moist

3 tbsp olive oil
400g baby onions, peeled and left whole
3 garlic cloves, finely sliced

3 tbsp balsamic vinegar
freshly ground black pepper
a drizzle of olive oil
or chilli oil, to serve

1 Preheat the oven to 180°C/160°C fan/gas 4. Heat the oil in a deep frying pan over a low heat, add the onions and cook, stirring frequently, for 15 minutes, or until evenly golden.

2 Transfer the onions to a small baking dish, packing them in tightly. Sprinkle with the garlic and spoon over the balsamic vinegar. Season well with black pepper, and bake for 20 minutes, stirring every 5 minutes. Serve hot or cold with a drizzle of olive oil or chilli oil.

**Per serving** 545kJ/131kcal (7%), 7.8g fat (11%), 1.1g saturates (6%), 10.2g sugars (11%), <0.01g salt (<1%)

**Why not try?**
Use **225g baby leeks** instead of the baby onions. Fry them in **45g butter** instead of the oil for 2 minutes, turning once or twice until lightly golden and softening. Transfer to a baking dish and add a small handful of **chopped walnuts**, a **bay leaf** and **3 tbsp white condiment vinegar** instead of the balsamic vinegar. Season with black pepper. Cook as before and serve hot or cold.

# Griddled sweet potato and celeriac

This simple combination of vegetables makes a lovely winter side dish and is a delicious accompaniment to both roast meats and casseroles

2 small or 1 large celeriac, cut in half if small, quarters if large, and then sliced

2–3 sweet potatoes, peeled and cut into 5mm thick slices

½ tsp sunflower oil

freshly ground black pepper

a pinch of paprika (optional)

1 Preheat a griddle pan. Brush the vegetables with oil on both sides, season with black pepper and dust lightly with paprika, if using.

2 When the griddle is very hot, but not smoking, add a single layer of vegetables (don't overcrowd them). Press them down firmly with a fish slice until the undersides are nicely striped. Turn the vegetables over and cook for a further 2–3 minutes until just cooked and striped. Don't overcook them, or they will become too soft.

3 Once the batch of vegetables are cooked until striped and just tender, transfer to a warm place, keeping them covered, while you cook the rest of the slices, reheating the griddle between each batch. Then serve all the slices piping hot.

**Per serving** 398kJ/95kcal (5%), 1.2g fat (2%), <0.1g saturates (<1%), 5.6g sugars (6%), 0.39g salt (7%)

# Sage and onion stuffing balls

Cooking the stuffing separately from the meat gives it a crispy exterior

butter, for greasing

1 tbsp olive oil

1 large onion, very finely chopped

100g fresh white breadcrumbs

2 tbsp finely chopped sage leaves

freshly ground black pepper

1 egg, lightly beaten

1 Preheat the oven to 180°C/160°C fan/gas 4. Grease a medium, shallow, ovenproof dish with butter.

2 Heat the oil in a saucepan over a medium heat, cover and gently fry the onion for 10 minutes. Leave to cool.

3 Stir in the breadcrumbs, sage and black pepper. Add the egg and stir.

4 Using your hands, form the stuffing into 8 equal-sized balls. Place in the greased dish and bake for 20-25 minutes.

**Per serving** 687kJ/163kcal (8%), 5.4g fat (8%), 1.4g saturates (7%), 2.8g sugars (3%), 0.53g salt (9%)

SERVES 4
PREP 10 minutes
COOK 1 hour 10 minutes

# Roast potatoes

Roast potatoes are a completely indispensable component
of a Sunday roast

1kg white potatoes, such as
Desiree or Maris Piper, peeled
and halved
1½ tbsp vegetable oil

1  Preheat the oven to 200°C/180°C fan/gas 6. Bring the potatoes to the boil in a large
pan of water. Reduce the heat to a brisk simmer and cook, uncovered, for 10 minutes until
softening at the edges. Drain, return to the pan and place over a low heat for a minute to
remove excess water, then remove from the heat, cover and shake to rough up the edges.

2  Meanwhile, put the oil in a roasting tin big enough to take the potatoes in a single layer.
Heat in the oven for 5 minutes.

3  Carefully remove the pan from the oven and add the potatoes. Turn to coat in the oil,
then spread out. Roast for 45 minutes–1 hour, turning them once they have formed
a crust underneath.

**Per serving** 1011kJ/240kcal (12%), 4.3g fat (6%), 0.3g saturates (2%),
1.5g sugars (2%), 0.04g salt (<1%)

# Desserts

# Black cherry cheesecake

This cheesecake is easy to assemble and makes an impressive-looking dessert

125g Basics digestive biscuits by Sainsbury's
50g sunflower spread
400g lighter soft cheese by Sainsbury's
75g golden caster sugar

4 lemons, zest and juice
150ml whipping cream
12g sachet powdered gelatine
425g tin pitted black cherries in light syrup by Sainsbury's

1 Grease and line a 20cm springform cake tin. Put the biscuits into a freezer bag and crush them using a rolling pin. Melt the sunflower spread in a pan, add the biscuits and stir until well coated. Transfer the mixture to the tin, pressing it down firmly with the back of a spoon so that it is level.

2 Mix the soft cheese, sugar and lemon zest together in a bowl. Put the cream in a bowl and whip lightly with a hand whisk until it forms soft peaks. Add to the soft cheese mixture and beat with a wooden spoon until well combined.

3 Mix the lemon juice and gelatine in a small heatproof bowl, then sit the bowl over a pan of simmering water and stir until the gelatine dissolves. Add to the cheese mixture and stir well. Pour the mixture on top of the biscuits, spreading it out evenly. Cover and place in the fridge for a couple of hours, or until set and firm.

4 Meanwhile, drain the cherries, reserving the syrup. Once the cheesecake is set, pile the cherries on top of it, spoon over the syrup and serve.

**Per serving** 1152kJ/276kcal (14%), 16.4g fat (23%), 8.6g saturates (43%), 18.6g sugars (21%), 0.44g salt (7%)

# Raspberry and white chocolate trifle

Tart raspberries contrast well with sweet white chocolate, and a trickle of cassis liqueur transforms this dessert into an indulgent, special occasion trifle

200g bar Fairtrade white chocolate by Sainsbury's, broken into even-sized pieces, 10g reserved and grated, to decorate
175g amaretti biscuits, crumbled
1–2 oranges, juice only

300ml whipping cream, lightly whipped
1 tbsp cassis (optional)
300g raspberries
15g flaked almonds, lightly toasted

**1** Put the chocolate in a heatproof bowl over a pan of barely simmering water and stir occasionally until melted, ensuring that the bowl does not touch the water. Remove the bowl from the pan and leave to cool slightly.

**2** Place the crumbled amaretti biscuits in the base of a glass serving dish. Pour over just enough orange juice to wet the biscuits. Set aside to allow the biscuits to absorb the juice.

**3** Mix the melted chocolate with half the whipped cream and stir well to combine. Mix the cassis (if using) with the raspberries. Reserve some raspberries for decoration. Spoon half the cream mixture into the dish and top with half the raspberry mixture. Repeat the layers to use the remaining cream and raspberry mixture. Top with the leftover cream and dot with the reserved raspberries, then sprinkle over the almonds and grated white chocolate. Chill before serving.

**Per serving** 1697kJ/408kcal (20%), 26.8g fat (38%), 15.3g saturates (77%), 33.6g sugars (37%), 0.15g salt (3%)

## Cook's tip
A variety of bases can be used for the trifle – try brownies, biscuits or fruit cake, instead of the amaretti for a heavier version – and try stewed fruits, instead of raspberries, for a winter pudding.

# Tiramisu

This delicious Italian dessert has many versions. The name means 'pick me up'. To be truly authentic, use espresso coffee

**FOR THE MASCARPONE MIXTURE**
250g lighter mascarpone by Sainsbury's
1 tsp vanilla extract
4 tbsp caster sugar
400ml single cream

**FOR THE SPONGE LAYERS**
150ml espresso coffee or 1½ tbsp instant coffee made up with boiling water

3 tbsp Tia Maria or Kahlúa (coffee liqueur)
3 tbsp brandy
200g pack Taste the Difference Italian Savoiardi sponge fingers by Sainsbury's, split lenghtways

**TO SERVE**
1 tbsp cocoa powder
1 tbsp espresso coffee powder

**1** Mix together the mascarpone, vanilla extract, sugar and cream in a large bowl.

**2** Combine the espresso, Tia Maria and brandy in a shallow dish. Dip each of the sponge fingers, cut-side down, in the coffee mixture.

**3** Place enough sponge fingers in the bottom of a 26 x 21cm rectangular serving dish to make a single layer. Sprinkle with 2 tablespoons of the remaining coffee mixture.

**4** Spoon half of the mascarpone mixture over the sponge fingers to cover them completely. Continue layering the moistened sponge fingers and mascarpone mixture, ending with a layer of mascarpone.

**5** Smooth the surface with a large metal spoon. Cover and chill for at least 6 hours.

**6** Mix together the cocoa and coffee powders. Sift them over the top of the tiramisu and serve.

**Per serving** 1072kJ/256kcal (13%), 13.5g fat (19%), 7.8g saturates (39%), 19.8g sugars (22%), 0.11g salt (2%)

### Get ahead
This can be assembled up to 2 days ahead and kept, covered, in the fridge. Add the cocoa and coffee powders just before serving.

# Apple pie

British Bramley apples are the best apples to use for this family favourite

250g self-raising flour
50g icing sugar
125g baking block by
Sainsbury's, cubed
1 large egg, beaten, plus
extra for glazing
2 tsp semi-skimmed milk
4 Bramley apples, peeled,
cored and sliced

1 tbsp cornflour
1 lemon, zest and juice
50g granulated sugar
$\frac{1}{2}$ tsp ground ginger
$\frac{1}{2}$ tsp ground cinnamon
4 scoops Be good to yourself
vanilla ice cream by Sainsbury's,
to serve

1 Pulse the flour, icing sugar and baking block in a food processor until it resembles breadcrumbs. Add the egg and pulse until the dough comes together in a smooth ball, adding the milk if necessary. Wrap in cling film and chill in the fridge.

2 Meanwhile, in a bowl, mix together the apples, cornflour, lemon zest and juice, sugar and spices. Place in a 1 litre ovenproof dish and brush the edges with a little beaten egg. Preheat the oven to 190°C/170°C fan/gas 5.

3 Roll out the pastry to 0.5cm thickness. Place over the apple mixture and pinch the edges to secure to the rim. Trim the edges with a sharp knife. Make a small hole in the centre. Gather the excess pastry, roll out and cut into strips. Decorate the top of the pie in a trellis design, using the beaten egg to secure the strips in place.

4 Brush the top with beaten egg and bake for 20 minutes. Reduce the oven to 180°C/160°C fan/gas 4 and bake for a further 15-20 minutes until golden. Serve warm or cold with a small scoop of ice cream.

**Per serving** 2910kJ/693kcal (36%), 28g fat (40%), 10.5g saturates (53%), 43.8g sugars (49%), 0.98g salt (16%)

# Apricot tart

This classic French tart is filled with a delicate custard and juicy apricots and makes a delicious dessert

**FOR THE PASTRY**
175g plain flour, plus
extra for dusting
25g caster sugar
100g baking block,
cut into pieces
1 egg, separated

**FOR THE FILLING**
200ml single cream
50g caster sugar
2 eggs, plus 1 egg yolk
½ tsp Madagascan vanilla
extract by Sainsbury's

411g tin apricot halves in fruit
juice by Sainsbury's, drained

**1** To make the pastry, rub the flour, sugar and baking block together with your fingertips, or pulse-blend in a food processor, until the mixture resembles fine crumbs. Add the egg yolk and enough water to form a soft dough. Wrap and chill for 30 minutes. Preheat the oven to 180°C/160°C fan/gas 4.

**2** Roll out the pastry on a floured surface to 3mm thick and use to line a 22cm loose-bottomed tart tin, leaving an overhang of at least 1cm. Prick with a fork, brush with the egg white to seal, line with greaseproof & non-stick baking paper by Sainsbury's and fill with baking beans. Bake for 20 minutes. Remove the beans and paper, and bake for a further 5 minutes. Trim off the ragged edges while warm with a sharp knife.

**3** For the filling, whisk the cream, sugar, eggs, yolk and vanilla in a bowl. Lay the apricots, cut-sides down, over the tart case. Place on a baking tray and pour the cream mixture over the fruit. Bake for 30–35 minutes until just set. Allow to cool to room temperature before serving.

**Per serving** 1266kJ/303kcal (15%), 16.7g fat (24%), 7.1g saturates (36%), 14.9g sugars (17%), 0.25g salt (4%)

**Get ahead**
This pastry case can be wrapped well in cling film, then sealed with foil and frozen for up to 12 weeks. Defrost thoroughly before use.

# Chocolate espresso pots

These little chocolate pots taste deliciously wicked, but in fact a little chocolate goes a long way and the silky texture comes without any cream being added

410g tin prunes unsweetened
in juice by Sainsbury's
150g dark Fairtrade chocolate
by Sainsbury's, broken into
small pieces

2 eggs, separated
25g pistachio nuts, finely
chopped, to serve

**1** Strain the prunes, reserving the juice, then press each prune gently between your fingers to eject the stone. Tip the prunes into a food processor or blender with 100ml of the reserved juice, adding a little extra water if necessary, to make up the liquid. Process to a purée.

**2** Melt the chocolate in a small heatproof bowl set over a pan of simmering water. Stir in the prune mixture and egg yolks.

**3** In a large, clean bowl, whisk the egg whites until they form stiff peaks. Fold the egg whites into the chocolate mixture using a large metal spoon.

**4** Spoon the chocolate mixture into 8 espresso cups or individual serving dishes. Cover the pots and refrigerate for at least 1 hour.

**5** Remove from the fridge just before serving and scatter with a few chopped pistachio nuts.

**Per serving** 703kJ/168kcal (8%), 9.1g fat (13%), 4.5g saturates (23%), 13.6g sugars (15%), 0.07g salt (1%)

**SERVES** 8
**PREP** 30 minutes,
plus chilling
**COOK** 25-30 minutes

# Fruit galette

Top these delicious puff pastries with whatever seasonal fruit
you fancy; apricots work particularly well

100g golden marzipan
by Sainsbury's
3 pears
2 tbsp lemon juice
375g pack ready rolled light
puff pastry by Sainsbury's
plain flour, for dusting

6 plums, quartered
and stoned
caster sugar, for sprinkling
15g flaked almonds
milk, for glazing
1 tsp icing sugar, for dusting

**1** To prepare the filling, coarsely grate the marzipan. Peel, quarter, core and thinly slice
the pears, then toss in a little lemon juice.

**2** Preheat the oven to 220°C/200°C fan/gas 7. Cut the pastry into 8 equal rectangles.
Place well apart on a baking sheet.

**3** Leaving a 1cm border all around the edges, scatter a little marzipan in the centre of
each tart, top half with the pear slices and the others with plum quarters. Brush with
the remaining lemon juice, then sprinkle with caster sugar and almonds. Brush the
pastry edges with milk and bake for 25-30 minutes, or until the pastry is golden
and puffy around the edges. Serve dusted with icing sugar.

**Per serving** 1143kJ/272kcal (14%), 10.5g fat (15%), 3.7g saturates (19%),
20.1g sugars (22%), 0.29g salt (5%)

## Cook's tip
Use a sweet dessert pear for this recipe, but
try to pick one that's slightly underripe, as
these are better for baking.

**MAKES** 12
**PREP** 15 minutes,
plus cooling
**COOK** 15 minutes

# Banana, cinnamon and pistachio parcels

These quick and easy parcels pair bananas with filo pastry and pistachios

4 small, ripe bananas, peeled and thickly sliced

30g pistachio nuts, chopped, plus extra to serve

1 ½ tbsp caster sugar

1 lemon, grated zest

¼ tsp ground cinnamon

50g sunflower spread, plus extra for brushing

220g ready rolled filo pastry by Sainsbury's

1  Place the bananas and pistachio nuts in a bowl and sprinkle with the sugar, lemon zest and cinnamon. Melt the sunflower spread in a small pan, add 4 tablespoons to the banana mixture and mix well.

2  Preheat the oven to 200ºC/180ºC fan/gas 6. Melt the remaining sunflower spread. Lay one sheet of filo pastry on the work surface, brush lightly with melted sunflower spread and then fold 3 times, lengthways, to make a long rectangle.

3  Heap a tablespoonful of the banana mixture onto the pastry about 4cm from the end. Fold the left corner of the pastry diagonally to the right side of the dough, to cover the filling. Then fold the right corner diagonally to the left, and continue folding alternate corners in the same way until you reach the end of the sheet, forming a little parcel. Repeat with the remaining sheets of filo pastry to make 12 parcels.

4  Place the parcels on a lightly greased baking sheet, brush with a little more melted sunflower spread and bake for 15 minutes, or until golden. Sprinkle with a few chopped pistachio nuts before serving.

**Per serving** 633kJ/151kcal (8%), 7g fat (10%), 1.4g saturates (7%), 7.7g sugars (9%), 0.28g salt (5%)

# Creamy rice pudding

So different from the taste of ready-made rice pudding, it's worth making the effort to make your own, particularly if you have the oven on for a roast

20g unsalted butter
100g pudding rice by Sainsbury's
50g Fairtrade golden caster sugar by Sainsbury's
1 litre semi-skimmed milk
75ml single cream
grated nutmeg, to taste

4 tsp Taste the Difference Bramley apple and berry compôte by Sainsbury's, to serve

1 Preheat the oven to 140°C/120°C fan/gas 1. Melt the butter in a medium flameproof casserole over a low heat.

2 Add the rice to the dish and stir well to coat in the butter. Stir the sugar into the rice and pour in the milk and cream. Stir well to combine.

3 Gradually bring the mixture to a simmer over a medium heat, stirring constantly. Sprinkle nutmeg over, cover and bake in the oven for 2 hours. Set aside to rest for 20 minutes before serving with the compôte.

**Per serving** 975kJ/232kcal (12%), 8.2g fat (12%), 4.9g saturates (25%), 18.7g sugars (21%), 0.29g salt (5%)

**Why not try?**
For an extra treat, stir in a handful of dark, white or milk chocolate chips. For added flavour and texture, stir in 50g dried fruit, such as sultanas, chopped apricots, figs or prunes and 1/2 tsp ground cinnamon, just before resting in step 3.

# Roasted figs with citrus crème fraîche

A simple dessert with 'wow factor' flavour, this dish takes
no time at all to prepare

8 fresh figs, stalks snipped
2 oranges, juice only
2 tsp caster sugar
pinch of ground cinnamon

150g half-fat crème fraîche
by Sainsbury's
½ lime, zest and juice

**1** Preheat the oven to 200°C/180°C fan/gas 6. Make a cross at the top of each fig and
gently squeeze the fruit apart a little. Place the figs in an ovenproof dish.

**2** Pour in the orange juice, and sprinkle with the sugar and cinnamon. Put in the oven
to cook for about 15 minutes until the figs have softened and are beginning to caramelize.

**3** Mix the crème fraîche with the lime juice and zest, and spoon it over the figs in the
dish. Serve immediately.

**Per serving** 1043kJ/248kcal (12%), 6.7g fat (10%), 3.8g saturates (19%),
40g sugars (44%), 0.09g salt (2%)

**Cook's tip**
For a special occasion, you could drizzle a tiny amount
of cassis over the figs before roasting.

# Cherry strudel

Sweet, softened cherries pair wonderfully with crunchy, nutty pastry in this classic Austrian dessert

35g fresh breadcrumbs

30g caster sugar

20g ground almonds

425g tin pitted black cherries in light syrup by Sainsbury's, drained and halved, or 325g fresh cherries, pitted and halved

1 orange, finely grated zest only

½ lemon, juice only

220g pack ready-rolled filo pastry by Sainsbury's

25g unsalted butter, melted, plus a little extra for brushing

½ tsp ground cinnamon

20g walnuts, ground in food processor

1 tbsp flaked almonds

icing sugar, for dusting

1 To make the filling, mix the breadcrumbs, caster sugar and ground almonds together in a bowl and set aside. In a second bowl, toss the cherries with the orange zest and lemon juice, cover and set aside.

2 Preheat the oven to 190°C/170°C fan/gas 5. Arrange a sheet of greaseproof & non-stick baking paper by Sainsbury's on a flat surface. Lay a sheet of filo pastry on the baking paper, with one of the longer edges of the pastry rectangle facing you. Brush the surface of the pastry with some of the melted butter and sprinkle over a little of the cinnamon. Repeat with the rest of the pastry sheets, butter and cinnamon.

3 Scatter the breadcrumb filling over the pastry stack, leaving a 5cm border around the edge (this will help when you fold the pastry edges over to prevent the filling escaping). If you want to make 2 strudels, cut the pastry in half, leaving a 10cm space in the middle. Scatter the ground walnuts over the filling and heap the cherries in a thick strip along the centre of the pastry, leaving a 5cm gap at either end.

4 Fold in the short edges of the pastry rectangle. Then, using the baking paper, fold over the long edge of the pastry rectangle nearest you, and roll up the pastry to enclose the filling and create a long roll. Brush the surface of the rolled pastry with more melted butter and scatter over the flaked almonds.

5 Lift the baking parchment with the strudel, seam-side down, onto a large baking sheet and bake in the oven for 30 minutes, or until the pastry is golden. Allow to cool for about 10 minutes, then dust with icing sugar and serve.

**Per serving** 1037kJ/247kcal (12%), 8.8g fat (13%), 2.5g saturates (13%), 10.4g sugars (12%), 0.44g salt (7%)

# Bakewell tart

With its frangipane topping, this indulgent version of the English teatime classic can also be served warm as a dessert

150g plain flour, sifted, plus extra for dusting
100g baking block by Sainsbury's, chilled and diced
50g caster sugar
½ lemon, grated zest
1 egg yolk
½ tsp Madagascan vanilla extract by Sainsbury's

**FOR THE FILLING**
125g unsalted butter, softened
125g caster sugar
3 large eggs
½ tsp Taste the Difference French bitter almond extract by Sainsbury's
125g ground almonds

150g Taste the Difference raspberry conserve by Sainsbury's
25g flaked almonds
icing sugar, to serve

1 Rub together the flour and baking block with your fingers, or pulse-blend in a food processor, to form fine crumbs. Stir in the sugar and lemon zest. Beat the egg yolk with the vanilla extract and mix into the crumbs, bringing the mixture together to form a soft dough; add a little water, if needed. Wrap the dough in cling film and refrigerate for 1 hour.

2 Preheat the oven to 180°C/160°C fan/gas 4. Roll the dough out on a floured surface to a thickness of about 3mm. It will be quite fragile, so if it begins to crumble, bring it together with your hands and give it a gentle knead to get rid of any joins. Use it to line a 24cm loose-bottomed tart tin, leaving an overlapping edge of at least 2cm. Prick the base all over with a fork. Line the pastry case with parchment and top with the baking beans.

3 Place the case on a baking sheet and blind bake it for 20 minutes. Remove the beans and the paper, and return it to the oven for another 5 minutes, if the centre still looks a little uncooked.

4 To make the filling, cream together the butter and sugar until pale and fluffy. Beat in the eggs and almond extract until well combined. Fold in the ground almonds to form a thick paste.

5 Spread the conserve over the base of the cooked tart case. Tip the almond mixture over the conserve layer and use a palette knife to spread it out evenly. Scatter the flaked almonds over the top.

6 Bake in the centre of the oven for 40 minutes until golden. Remove from the oven and allow to cool for 5 minutes. Then take a small, sharp knife and use it to trim the excess pastry from the edges of the tart, taking care to cut down and away from the tart so no crumbs fall on the surface. Allow the tart to cool before dusting with icing sugar to serve.

**Per serving** 2034kJ/487kcal (24%), 27.6g fat (39%), 6.5g saturates (33%), 34.4g sugars (38%), 0.47g salt (8%)

# Berry and banana crumble

A crumble makes a tasty family treat – this one contains the unusual mixture of banana and berries, with an extra crunch from flaked almonds

400g frozen summer fruits
by Sainsbury's
2 bananas, thickly sliced
100g plain flour, sifted
100g baking block, chilled
and cut into cubes

50g jumbo oats
50g Fairtrade caster sugar
by Sainsbury's
40g flaked almonds

1 Preheat the oven to 180°C/160°C fan/gas 4. Place all the fruit in a medium baking dish.

2 Put the flour in a large mixing bowl and rub in the baking block with your fingertips until the mixture resembles coarse breadcrumbs. Stir in the oats, sugar and almonds.

3 Sprinkle the crumble mixture over the fruit and use the back of a metal spoon to smooth it into an even layer.

4 Place the dish on a baking tray and bake for 30-40 minutes, or until golden.

**Per serving** 1319kJ/316kcal (16%), 17.1g fat (24%), 5.1g saturates (26%), 19.4g sugars (22%), 0.19g salt (3%)

**Why not try?**
Try adding 3 tbsp of chopped pecan nuts or walnuts to this topping, or stir in ½ tsp of ground cinnamon.

# Cakes
# and bakes

**SERVES** 12
**PREP** 55 minutes
**COOK** 40 minutes

# Black Forest gâteau

Ever popular, this retro German cake is a favourite for celebrations.
A little of this cake goes a long way

85g baking block, melted,
plus extra for greasing
6 eggs
150g Fairtrade golden caster
sugar by Sainsbury's
125g plain flour
50g cocoa powder
1 tsp Madagascan vanilla
extract by Sainsbury's

**FOR THE FILLING
AND DECORATION**
2 x 425g tins pitted black
cherries in light syrup by
Sainsbury's, drained, 6 tbsp
syrup reserved, and cherries
from 1 tin roughly chopped

4 tbsp Taste the Difference
Kirsch by Sainsbury's
500ml whipping cream
15g dark chocolate, grated

**1** Preheat the oven to 180°C/160°C fan/gas 4. Grease and line a 23cm round springform cake tin with greaseproof & non-stick baking paper by Sainsbury's.

**2** Put the eggs and sugar into a large heatproof bowl that will fit over a saucepan. Place the bowl over a pan of simmering water. Don't let the bowl touch the water. Whisk until the mixture is pale and thick and will hold a trail from the beaters. Remove from the heat and whisk for another 5 minutes, or until cooled slightly.

**3** Sift the flour and cocoa together, and gently fold into the egg mixture using a spatula. Then fold in the vanilla and baking block. Transfer to the prepared tin and level the surface. Bake in the oven for 40 minutes, or until risen and just shrinking away from the sides. Turn out onto a wire rack, discard the paper and cover with a clean cloth. Let it cool.

**4** Carefully cut the cake into 3 layers, using a serrated knife and long sweeping strokes. Combine the reserved cherry juice with the Kirsch, and drizzle a third over each layer.

**5** Whip the cream in a separate bowl until it just holds its shape; it should not be too stiff. Place a layer of cake on a plate. Spread with cream and half the chopped cherries. Repeat with the second sponge. Top with the final sponge, baked side up. Press down. Cover the side with a layer of cream. Put the remaining cream in the piping bag.

**6** Press grated chocolate onto the creamy sides with a palette knife. Pipe a ring of cream swirls around the cake and place the whole cherries inside. Sprinkle any remaining chocolate evenly over the peaks of piped cream, to serve.

**Per serving** 1694kJ/406kcal (20%), 25.8g fat (37%), 13.6g saturates (68%), 27.2g sugars (30%), 0.2g salt (3%)

**Get ahead**
The cake can be covered and chilled for up to 3 days before decorating.

**SERVES** 12
**PREP** 35 minutes, plus overnight soaking, resting and rising
**COOK** 50 minutes

# Stollen

This fruity yeast bread, originally from Germany, is traditionally served at Christmas and makes a great alternative to Christmas cake or mince pies

200g raisins

100g currants

100ml Basics dark rum by Sainsbury's

400g plain flour, plus extra for dusting

7g sachet fast action dried yeast by Sainsbury's

60g caster sugar

100ml semi-skimmed milk

few drops of pure vanilla extract

pinch of salt

½ tsp ground mixed spice

2 eggs

175g baking block by Sainsbury's

200g mixed candied peel

100g ground almonds

icing sugar, for dusting

1  Put the raisins and currants into a bowl, pour over the rum and leave to soak overnight.

2  The following day, sift the flour into a large bowl, make a well in the centre, sprinkle in the yeast and add 1 teaspoon of the sugar. Gently heat the milk until lukewarm, and pour on top of the yeast. Leave to stand at room temperature for 15 minutes, or until frothy.

3  Add the rest of the sugar, the vanilla extract, salt, mixed spice, eggs and baking block. Using a wooden spoon, or mixer with a dough hook, mix, then knead the ingredients together for 5 minutes, or until they form a smooth dough.

4  Transfer to a lightly floured work surface. Add the candied peel, soaked raisins and currants, and ground almonds to the dough, kneading for a few minutes, or until evenly incorporated. Return the dough to the bowl, cover with cling film or a damp tea towel and leave to rise in a warm place until it has doubled in size.

5  Preheat the oven to 160°C/140°C fan/gas 3. Line an oven tray with greaseproof & non-stick baking paper by Sainsbury's. On a floured surface, roll out the dough to make a 30 x 25cm rectangle. Fold 1 long side over, just beyond the middle, then fold over the other long side to overlap the first, curling it over slightly on top to create the stollen shape. Transfer to the oven tray, and put in a warm place to rise again until doubled in size.

6  Bake in the oven for 50 minutes, or until risen and pale golden. Transfer to a wire rack to cool completely, then dust with icing sugar. Serve cut into slices.

**Per serving** 1834kJ/437kcal (22%), 17.3g fat (25%), 4.8g saturates (24%), 35.9g sugars (40%), 0.36g salt (6%)

Get ahead
Freeze the stollen for up to 1 month; thaw overnight and dust with icing sugar before serving.

SERVES 26
PREP 25 minutes, plus soaking
COOK 2 hours 30 minutes

# Rich fruit cake

A wonderfully moist, rich cake. For large celebrations, bake in a square tin for easy portioning

200g sultanas
400g raisins
350g prunes, pitted if necessary, chopped
350g glacé cherries
2 apples, peeled, cored and diced
600ml Original Somerset cider by Sainsbury's

4 tsp mixed spice
200g unsalted butter, softened
175g Fairtrade dark soft brown sugar by Sainsbury's
3 eggs, lightly beaten
150g ground almonds
280g plain flour, plus extra for dusting
2 tsp baking powder

454g pack golden marzipan by Sainsbury's
2 tbsp apricot jam
3 large egg whites
500g icing sugar

1 Place the sultanas, raisins, prunes, cherries, apples, cider and spice in a pan. Bring to a simmer over a medium-low heat, then cover for 20 minutes until most of the liquid is absorbed. Cover and leave overnight so that the fruits absorb the liquid.

2 Preheat the oven to 140°C/120°C fan/gas 1. Double-line a 25cm deep round cake tin with greaseproof & non-stick baking paper by Sainsbury's.

3 Whisk the butter and sugar using an electric hand-held whisk in a bowl until fluffy. Add the eggs, a little at a time, beating well after each addition.

4 Gently fold in the fruit mix and ground almonds, to maintain volume. Sift the flour and baking powder and gently fold into the mixture. Transfer into the tin, cover with foil and bake for 2 hours 30 minutes until a skewer inserted into the centre comes out clean. If the top is browning quickly and the insides are not quite cooked, place a folded piece of greaseproof paper on the top and bake for slightly longer, testing again with the skewer.

5 Leave the cake to cool, then turn out onto a wire rack to cool completely. Remove the baking paper and trim the cake to level it. Transfer to a stand and hold it in place with a small ball of marzipan.

6 Warm the jam and brush over the cake. On a lightly floured surface, knead the remaining marzipan until softened and roll out until wide enough to cover the cake completely. Drape the marzipan over the rolling pin and place it over the cake. Gently ease the marzipan into place, smoothing out any bumps. Cut away excess marzipan from the base of the cake.

7 To make the icing, place the egg whites in a bowl and sift in the icing sugar, stirring well to combine. Whisk for 10 minutes using an electric hand-held whisk until stiff. Spread the icing over the cake and leave covered overnight to set before serving.

Per serving 2002kJ/475kcal (24%), 13.0g fat (19%), 4.5g saturates (23%), 71.2g sugars (79%), 0.1g salt (2%)

**SERVES** 10
**PREP** 15 minutes, plus
soaking and proving
**COOK** 50 minutes

# Barmbrack

This bread is of Irish origin, where it is sometimes served for Hallowe'en with little charms in it, which are supposed to forecast your luck for the following year

500g mixed dried fruit
125ml hot, strong black tea
500g strong plain flour, plus extra for dusting
75g unsalted butter, plus extra for greasing

75g caster sugar
1½ tsp ground mixed spice
7g sachet fast action dried yeast by Sainsbury's
½ tsp salt

150ml semi-skimmed milk, lukewarm
1 medium egg, plus 1 medium egg, for glazing

**1** Put the dried fruit into a bowl and pour the tea onto the fruit. Stir, then cover the bowl and leave the fruit to soak in and absorb the tea, for at least 2 hours, or overnight.

**2** Put the flour into a bowl and rub in the butter until the mixture resembles fine breadcrumbs. Stir in the sugar, spice, yeast and salt, and create a well in the centre. Lightly beat together the milk and egg, and gradually pour into the well in the flour mixture, and stir to bring the mixture together. If the mixture is too sticky, add a little flour.

**3** Turn the dough out onto a lightly floured surface, and knead for 8-10 minutes, or until smooth and elastic. Add the fruit to the dough and knead until the fruit is well mixed, taking care not to knead too much or the soft fruit will start to break down. Depending on the fruit used, it may not have fully absorbed all the tea, and the excess tea may make the dough too sticky. If that happens add a little more flour. If you need to add a little more liquid, use a little of the tea used to soak the fruit.

**4** Lightly grease a 20cm round cake tin. Shape the dough into a ball, and press it into the tin. Cover the tin with a piece of oiled cling film, and leave it in a warm place for 40-60 minutes, or until the dough has doubled in size.

**5** Preheat the oven to 200°C/180°C fan/gas 6. Brush the top of the bread with beaten egg. Bake for 20 minutes. Reduce the temperature to 180°C/160°C fan/gas 4 and bake for a further 20-30 minutes, or until it sounds hollow when you take it out of the tin and tap it on the base. If the bread starts to colour too quickly, cover it with a sheet of foil.

**6** When the bread is cooked, remove it from the oven and transfer it to a wire rack to cool. Serve the bread warm or cold.

**Per serving** 1790kJ/424kcal (21%), 8.5g fat (12%), 4.6g saturates (23%), 42.7g sugars (47%), 0.25g salt (4%)

> **Cook's tip**
> You can freeze this bread for up to 1 month.
> Defrost thoroughly before serving.

**SERVES** 12
**PREP** 20 minutes
**COOK** 20 minutes

# Banana and oatmeal muffins

These muffins are a tasty choice for a late leisurely brunch or afternoon tea. They can be eaten when they are still warm

160g plain flour
1 tsp bicarbonate of soda
1 tsp baking powder
1 tsp ground cinnamon
100g medium oatmeal
110g sunflower spread

100g Fairtrade demerara cane sugar by Sainsbury's
2 eggs, lightly beaten
3 ripe bananas, mashed
120ml semi-skimmed milk

1 Preheat the oven to 190°C/170°C fan/gas 5. Place 12 cupcake cases in a 12-hole muffin tin, or simply place the cases on an oven tray.

2 Sift the flour, bicarbonate of soda, baking powder, cinnamon and oatmeal into a large bowl. Tip in any bran left in the sieve. Stir well.

3 Place the sunflower spread and demerara sugar in a separate mixing bowl and cream together, using an electric hand-held whisk, until very light and fluffy. This could take up to 5 minutes. Add the eggs and mix well. Stir in the bananas and milk.

4 Pour the wet mixture into the dry and stir to combine. Do not over-mix or the muffins will be heavy. Divide the mixture between the cupcake cases.

5 Bake for 20 minutes (start checking after 15), or until a cocktail stick inserted into a muffin comes out clean. Transfer to a wire rack to cool.

**Per serving** 865kJ/206kcal (10%), 7.4g fat (11%), 1.7g saturates (9%), 14.3g sugars (16%), 0.5g salt (8%)

**MAKES** 20
**PREP** 20 minutes,
plus chilling
**COOK** 10-12 minutes

# Mince pies

Making your own mince pies is quick and easy. This homemade mincemeat is fruity, moist and full of flavour

1 small cooking apple
30g butter, melted
85g sultanas
85g raisins
55g currants
45g mixed peel, chopped
45g chopped almonds or hazelnuts
1 lemon, finely grated zest only

1 tsp mixed spice
1 tbsp brandy or whisky
30g soft dark brown muscovado sugar
1 small banana
500g ready rolled lighter shortcrust pastry by Sainsbury's
flour, for dusting
icing sugar, for dusting

**1** Preheat the oven to 190°C/170°C fan/gas 5. Grate the apple (including the skin), and place in a large bowl. Add the melted butter, sultanas, raisins, currants, mixed peel, nuts, lemon zest, mixed spice, brandy and sugar, and mix. Chop the banana into small dice, and add to the bowl. Mix well.

**2** Cut 18 rounds from the pastry using 7.5cm biscuit cutters. Cut a further 18 rounds or shapes using 6cm cutters.

**3** Line cupcake tins with the larger pastry rounds, and place a heaped teaspoon of mincemeat in each case. Top with the smaller rounds or shapes. Chill for 10 minutes, and then bake for 10-12 minutes, or until the pastry is golden. Carefully remove from the tins, and cool on a wire rack. Dust with icing sugar.

**Per serving** 753kJ/180kcal (9%), 7.8g fat (11%), 3.6g saturates (18%), 12.7g sugars (14%), 0.11g salt (2%)

### Get ahead
The pies can be baked up to 3 days in advance and stored in an airtight container.

# Victoria sponge cake

Probably the most iconic British cake, a good Victoria sponge should be well-risen, moist and as light as air

175g baking block, plus extra for greasing
175g caster sugar by Sainsbury's
3 eggs
1 tsp Madagascan vanilla extract by Sainsbury's

175g self-raising flour
1 tsp baking powder

**FOR THE FILLING**
50g unsalted butter, softened

100g icing sugar, plus extra for dusting
1 tsp Madagascan vanilla extract by Sainsbury's
115g seedless raspberry jam by Sainsbury's

1 Preheat the oven to 180°C/160°C fan/gas 4. Grease two 18cm round cake tins with baking block and line with greaseproof & non-stick baking paper by Sainsbury's.

2 Whisk the baking block and sugar in a bowl for 2 minutes, or until pale, light and fluffy. Add the eggs 1 at a time, mixing well between additions to avoid curdling. Add the vanilla extract, and whisk briefly until it is blended through. Whisk the mixture for another 2 minutes until bubbles appear on the surface. Remove the whisk, then sift the flour and baking powder into the bowl.

3 With a metal spoon, gently fold in the flour until just smooth; try to keep the mixture light. Divide the mixture evenly between the tins and level the tops with a palette knife. Cook for 20-25 minutes, or until golden and springy to the touch and a skewer inserted into the middle of the cakes comes out clean.

4 Remove from the oven and leave to cool for a few minutes in their tins. Turn them out, good sides up, onto a wire rack to cool completely.

5 To make the filling, beat the butter, icing sugar and vanilla extract until smooth. Continue to beat for up to 5 minutes until the buttercream is very light, cloud-like and fluffy in texture.

6 Spread the buttercream evenly onto the flat side of a cooled sponge with a palette knife. Gently spread the jam on top of the buttercream using a table knife. Top with the second sponge, so that the flat sides are together. Serve as soon as possible, dusted with sifted icing sugar.

**Per serving** 2024kJ/483kcal (24%), 24.3g fat (35%), 10g saturates (50%), 43.5g sugars (48%), 0.51g salt (9%)

### Cook's tip
Unfilled, the sponges will keep for up to 3 days in an airtight container. Separate with sheets of greaseproof paper, and keep away from heat and light. The just-cooled cakes can be wrapped in cling film, sealed with foil and kept frozen for up to 12 weeks. Defrost thoroughly before filling and serving.

SERVES 10
PREP 20 minutes
COOK 1 hour–1 hour
15 minutes

# Banana, date and walnut loaf

This classic combination of flavours is the perfect mix of sweet and mellow, just right for teatime

100g baking block by Sainsbury's
100g caster sugar by Sainsbury's
2 large eggs
225g self-raising flour, sifted

2 bananas, about 300g in total
100g stoned dates, chopped
50g walnut pieces, roughly chopped
1 tsp baking powder

1 Preheat the oven to 180°C/160°C fan/gas 4. Line a 900g loaf tin with greaseproof & non-stick baking paper by Sainsbury's.

2 Whisk the baking block and sugar in a bowl with an electric hand-held whisk until pale, light and fluffy. Add the eggs one at a time, beating well after each addition, and adding 1 tablespoon of the flour after each to prevent the mixture from curdling.

3 Peel and mash the bananas in a small bowl with a fork. Stir the mashed banana into the loaf mixture, along with the chopped dates and walnuts. Fold in the remaining flour and the baking powder, then transfer the mixture into the tin. Level the top, pressing well into the corners.

4 Bake for 1 hour–1 hour 15 minutes, or until risen and firm to the touch. If the top of the cake starts to colour too much before it is fully cooked, cover with foil. Leave to cool in the tin, cut into slices and serve.

**Per serving** 1202kJ/287kcal (14%), 12.5g fat (18%), 3.5g saturates (18%), 19.9g sugars (22%), 0.45g salt (8%)

**Love your leftovers**
For maximum sweetness, use up your over-ripe bananas with brown speckled skins in this recipe.

**SERVES** 8
**PREP** 15 minutes
**COOK** 20–25 minutes

# Quick carrot cake

Carrot cakes are ideal for novice bakers as they do not require lengthy whisking or delicate folding

75g sunflower spread, melted and cooled, plus extra for greasing
75g wholemeal self-raising flour
1 tsp ground allspice
½ tsp ground ginger
½ tsp baking powder
2 carrots, washed and coarsely grated
75g Fairtrade light soft brown sugar by Sainsbury's

50g sultanas
2 eggs, beaten
3 tbsp fresh orange juice

**FOR THE ICING**
150g light soft cheese by Sainsbury's, at room temperature
1 tbsp icing sugar
1 lemon, grated zest, to decorate

1 Preheat the oven to 190°C/170°C fan/gas 5. Grease a 20cm springform cake tin and line the base with greaseproof & non-stick baking paper by Sainsbury's.

2 Sift the flour, allspice, ginger and baking powder into a large bowl, tipping in any bran that remains in the sieve. Add the carrots, brown sugar and sultanas, then stir to mix. Add the eggs, 1 tablespoon of orange juice and the sunflower spread. Stir until blended.

3 Pour the cake mixture into the tin and level with a palette knife. Bake on a baking tray for 20 minutes or, until a skewer inserted into the centre of the cake comes out clean. Let it stand in the tin for 10 minutes to cool.

4 Run a knife around the sides, invert onto a wire rack, peel off the paper and leave to cool completely. Split the cake horizontally into 2 layers with a serrated knife.

5 For the icing, beat the cream cheese with the remaining orange juice and icing sugar. Spread the icing in the centre and over the top of the cake, and decorate with lemon zest.

**Per serving** 828kJ/198kcal (10%), 8.7g fat (12%), 2.9g saturates (15%), 18.8g sugars (21%), 0.36g salt (6%)

Get ahead
The cake will keep in an airtight container for 3 days.

**SERVES** 12
**PREP** 20 minutes
**COOK** 1 hour 15 minutes

# Courgette cake

Try this alternative to carrot cake. Don't be put off by the unusual inclusion of courgettes; they're less sweet than carrots, but add moisture and a fresh flavour

225ml sunflower oil, plus
extra for greasing
100g hazelnuts
3 large eggs
1 tsp Madagascan vanilla extract
by Sainsbury's
225g Fairtrade caster sugar
by Sainsbury's

200g courgettes, washed
and coarsely grated
200g self-raising flour
75g wholemeal self-raising flour
pinch of salt
1 tsp ground cinnamon
1 lemon, grated zest

**FOR THE ICING**
50g icing sugar
3–4 tsp lemon juice

**1** Preheat the oven to 180°C/160°C fan/gas 4. Oil the base and sides of a 900ml loaf tin and line the base with greaseproof & non-stick baking paper by Sainsbury's. Spread hazelnuts on an oven tray and cook for 5 minutes until lightly browned. Roughly chop and set aside, reserving a handful for decoration.

**2** Pour the oil and eggs into a bowl, add the vanilla and tip in the sugar. Whisk the oil mixture until lighter and thickened. Squeeze moisture from the courgettes using a clean tea towel. Fold together the courgettes and the nuts. Sift over the flours, tipping in any bran left in the sieve. Add the salt, cinnamon and lemon zest, and fold.

**3** Pour the mixture into the tin. Bake for 1 hour 15 minutes, or until springy to the touch. Turn out onto a wire rack to cool completely.

**4** For the icing, sift the icing sugar into a small bowl. Gradually add the lemon juice, stirring to make a smooth, thin icing.

**5** Drizzle the icing over the top of the cake and scatter over the reserved hazelnuts. Cut into slices and serve.

**Per serving** 1702kJ/408kcal (20%), 24.4g fat (35%), 2.9g saturates (15%), 23.8g sugars (26%), 0.32g salt (5%)

Get ahead
The cake will keep in an airtight container for 3 days.

# Oat and raisin cookies

These crisp, crumbly cookies are packed full of oats and sweet
raisins – perfect for a quick snack

150g baking block
by Sainsbury's
100g caster sugar
125g self-raising flour, sifted

100g jumbo porridge oats
50g Taste the Difference raisins
by Sainsbury's
1 tsp bicarbonate of soda

1 Preheat the oven to 180°C/160°C fan/gas 4. Melt the baking block in a large saucepan
over a gentle heat. Allow it to cool while you measure out the other ingredients.

2 Mix the sugar, flour, oats and raisins into the cooled, melted baking block and stir well.

3 In a cup, mix the bicarbonate of soda with 1 tablespoon of boiling water until it dissolves,
then mix it well into the biscuit mixture.

4 Take about 1 tablespoon of the mixture and roll it into a ball between your hands. Flatten
it slightly and put it on a baking tray. Repeat to use up all the dough, spacing them well
apart on the tray, as they will spread.

5 Bake in the centre of the oven for 12–15 minutes until they turn golden. Remove the
cookies from the oven and leave them to cool on their baking sheets for 5 minutes
to stop them breaking up, then transfer them to a wire rack to cool completely.

**Per serving** 555kJ/133kcal (7%), 7.7g fat (11%), 2.7g saturates (14%),
8.5g sugars (9%), 0.3g salt (5%)

MAKES 8
PREP 20 minutes
COOK 8-10 minutes

# Cheese and parsley scones

These tasty scones are made with an easy, savoury variation on the basic scone mix

oil, for greasing

225g plain flour, sifted, plus extra for dusting

1 tsp baking powder

50g sunflower spread

1 tsp dried parsley

1 tsp black peppercorns, crushed

50g mature Cheddar cheese by Sainsbury's, grated

150ml semi-skimmed milk

**1** Preheat the oven to 220°C/200°C fan/gas 7. Lightly oil a medium-sized baking sheet. In a large bowl, mix together the flour and baking powder. Add the sunflower spread, and using your fingertips, rub it in until the mixture resembles fine breadcrumbs.

**2** Stir in the parsley, black pepper and half the cheese. Then add enough milk to bind and make the dough come together (reserve the rest for brushing the tops of the scones). Lightly mix into a soft dough.

**3** Roll out the dough on a lightly floured surface to a thickness of about 2cm. Using a 6cm pastry cutter, cut out rounds (see Cook's tip, below). Sit them on the prepared baking sheet, brush with the remaining milk and sprinkle over the remaining cheese.

**4** Bake on the top shelf of the oven for 8-10 minutes until golden. Leave on the baking sheet for a couple of minutes to cool a little, then either serve warm or cool completely on a wire rack. These scones are best eaten the same day.

**Per serving** 797kJ/190kcal (10%), 8.5g fat (12%), 4.7g saturates (24%), 2.1g sugars (2%), 0.31g salt (5%)

### Cook's tip
One of the secrets to well-risen scones is in the way they are cut. It is best to use a sharp pastry cutter or knife, preferably made of metal. They should be cut with a strong downward motion, and the cutter should not be twisted at all when cutting. This helps create a high, even rise when cooking.

**SERVES** 10
**PREP** 20 minutes
**COOK** 30 minutes

# Lemon drizzle cake

The gloriously tangy lemon topping poured over the sponge produces a moist and mouthwatering cake

150g baking block by Sainsbury's
150g caster sugar by Sainsbury's
3 eggs
1 lemon, grated zest
150g self-raising flour, sifted

**FOR THE TOPPING**
3 tbsp lemon juice
60g caster sugar by Sainsbury's
icing sugar, for dusting

1 Preheat the oven to 180°C/160°C fan/gas 4. Line an 18cm round cake tin with greaseproof & non-stick baking paper by Sainsbury's.

2 In a large bowl, cream together the baking block and sugar with an electric hand-held whisk until light and fluffy. Whisk in the eggs one at a time, then add the zest.

3 Fold in the flour until just incorporated and pour the mixture into the tin. Bake in the centre of the preheated oven for 30 minutes until well risen and a skewer comes out clean.

4 To make the topping, gently heat the lemon juice and sugar in a small pan until the sugar has dissolved. Prick the cake all over with a thin wooden skewer and, leaving it in the tin, carefully pour the sugary mixture all over the top, a little at a time, until it has been absorbed. Allow the topping to cool before serving the cake, dusted with icing sugar.

**Per serving** 1106kJ/264kcal (13%), 12.9g fat (18%), 4.7g saturates (24%), 21.8g sugars (24%), 0.34g salt (6%)

**Why not try?**
Try replacing the lemon zest and juice with clementine or orange zest and juice. This version is especially welcome at Christmas.

Cakes and bakes

# Ten top tips

1 To test an egg for freshness, drop it in a bowl of cold water. If it sinks to the bottom and lies on its side, it's very fresh; if it sinks and rests on one end, it's fresh; and if floats, it's not fresh and should be discarded.

2 Don't overcrowd the pan, as this won't allow the food to cook evenly. If you've got a lot of food to cook, simply use two pans instead of one.

3 To help stop berries and dried fruit from sinking in a cake or bake, use a little of the flour from the recipe, and toss them in it before adding them to the mixture.

4 To avoid sauces getting lumpy, make sure that you add liquid to the flour little by little, and keep mixing all the time. If you still don't end up with a smooth sauce, simply sieve it to remove any lumps.

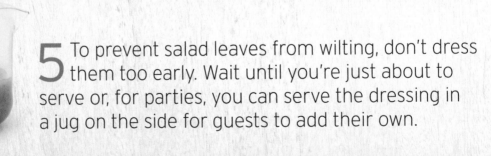

5 To prevent salad leaves from wilting, don't dress them too early. Wait until you're just about to serve or, for parties, you can serve the dressing in a jug on the side for guests to add their own.

6 Test whether meat is cooked using a meat thermometer, or by inserting a skewer into the thickest part of the joint; juices should run clear and there should be no pink remaining. Fish will be opaque and flake easily once cooked.

7 To ensure a crispy pizza base, preheat the oven with the baking tray inside, to allow it to heat up before you place the pizza on it. Making sure you sauté any watery vegetables, such as courgettes or mushrooms, before you add them to the pizza will also help prevent a soggy base.

8 Any traces of fat will stop egg whites from whipping properly, so ensure that no traces of yolk remain. Whip the eggs at room temperature in an absolutely clean bowl, wiping the bowl with the cut side of half a lemon to remove any remaining fat.

9 Pat meat dry before browning, otherwise the moisture will steam the meat, and it will not sear.

10 To stop home-frozen berries from becoming mushy when defrosted, freeze them overnight spread out on a tray, with individual berries not touching one another, before transferring them to freezer bags.

# Sainsbury's food safety advice

## General kitchen safety guidelines

● Wash your hands thoroughly before food preparation. If handling raw meat, fish or poultry, it's equally important to wash your hands after preparation, too.
● Keep raw food separate from ready-to-eat foods when you're preparing meals; use separate chopping boards and utensils or wash thoroughly between use.
● Washing raw chicken spreads bacteria around the kitchen via tiny splashes, which increases the risk of cross-contamination to other foods. The best way to destroy harmful bacteria is by cooking thoroughly, until piping hot throughout with no pink colour remaining in the flesh. Juices should also run clear when the thickest part of a joint is pierced with a skewer.
● Refer to ingredient packaging for full preparation and cooking instructions.
● Public health advice is to avoid eating raw or lightly cooked eggs, especially for those vulnerable to infections, including pregnant women, babies and the elderly.

● Wash fresh vegetables, fruit and herbs (including any used for garnishing dishes) before use.
● When reheating leftovers, make sure they are piping hot throughout.

## Freezing and defrosting

● Products can be frozen up to the use-by date (check labels to see if suitable for freezing).
● Defrost food overnight in the fridge (covered in a dish to avoid contaminating other products).

## Refrigerating food

● Keep your fridge temperature below 5ºC.
● To avoid cross-contamination, cover raw meat and poultry and store at the bottom of the fridge, separate from ready-to-eat food.
● When preparing food, keep out of the fridge for the shortest time possible.
● Cool down leftovers as quickly as possible then, once cooled, transfer them to the fridge and eat within 2 days.
● Clean your fridge regularly to ensure it remains hygienic and in good working condition.
● For tinned food, decant the contents into a non-metallic container.

## 'Best before' and 'use-by' dates

● Food with a 'best before' date is longer-lasting. It is safe to eat after this date but will not be at its best quality.
● Food with a 'use-by' date goes off quite quickly and what's more it could pose a health risk if consumed after this date.

## Deep frying

● When deep-frying, make sure that the pan is deep enough to avoid any splashes of hot oil.
● Ensure that the food is fully covered by the oil, with at least 1cm of oil above the food.
● Test if the oil is hot enough by dropping a piece of day old bread into the pan – it should brown quickly
● Keep small children and animals away from hot pans.
● Never leave a pan with hot oil in unattended.

## Recipe nutrition

The nutritional information on each recipe shown in this book has been calculated using Sainsbury's own-brand products and is based on 1 adult portion, assuming equal division of the recipe into the suggested number of servings.

Nutrition is calculated using each recipe's ingredients list only and does not include any sides, accompaniments or other serving suggestions mentioned in the method.
The nutrition content will vary if other products are used or if the servings are not identical. Also, variations in cooking methods may affect the nutritional content.

The nutritional information on each recipe also includes the percentage of Reference Intakes (RIs) provided by a serving. RIs are a guide to the maximum amounts of calories, fat, saturates, sugars and salt an adult should consume in a day (based on an average female adult) and are as on the right.

Seasoning: we're committed to promoting healthier eating and lowering salt in daily diets. As such we have worked hard to produce recipes that do not need as much (if any) salt seasoning. Note: recipe nutrition does not include any salt you add yourself.

| Energy or nutrient | Reference intake per day |
| --- | --- |
| Energy | 8400kJ/2000kcal |
| Total fat | 70g |
| Saturates | 20g |
| Total sugars | 90g |
| Salt | 6g |

For more information on food safety and nutrition, visit sainsburys.co.uk/livewellforless and sainsburys.co.uk/kitchensafety

# Index

# Credits

## DK UK
**Project Editor** Cressida Tuson
**Project Art Editor** Katherine Raj
**Managing Editors** Dawn Henderson,
Stephanie Farrow
**Managing Art Editor** Christine Keilty
**Editorial Assistant** Alice Kewellhampton
**Design Assistant** Laura Buscemi
**Senior Pre-Production Producer** Andy Hilliard
**Senior Producer** Kathleen McNally
**Creative Technical Support** Sonia Charbonnier
**Deputy Art Director** Maxine Pedliham
**Publisher** Peggy Vance
**Food Stylist** Jane Lawrie
**Prop Stylist** Morag Farquhar
**Photography** William Reavell

## DK India
**Assistant Art Editor** Gursimran Singh
**Art Editors** Aparajita Barai, Priyanka Singh
**DTP Designers** Anurag Trivedi, Satish Gaur
**Pre-Production Manager** Sunil Sharma
**Managing Art Editor** Navidita Thapa

## For Sainsbury's
**Book team** Mavis Sarfo, Lynne de Lacy,
Emma Brewster, Pete Selby, Iryna Peleno
**Nutrition** Johanna Hignett
**Product safety manager** Nikki Mosley,
Elizabeth Williamson

## Special thanks to
Seven Publishing for nutritional calculations
on the recipes, Kathy Steer for proofreading
and Vanessa Bird for the index.

Printed and bound by
Leo Paper Products Limited, China.

ISBN-13: 978-0-2411881-3-2

All the forest sources in this product have
been risk assessed for legality and responsible
management. To find out more about our values
and best practices go to **www.dk.com**